High Performance Sport Skill Instruction, Training, and Coaching

9 Powerful Principles for Athletes to Flow and Get in the Zone

DDJ Publishing

CONTENTS

INTRODUCTION

Are you a pro athlete in the making, but don't know how to make your way to the next level of your performance? Do you have all the talent required to excel in your sport but have no clue on how to hone your body and train your mind to the level needed to compete at the highest of levels? Well, I've got some great news for you, because that's exactly what I'm going to coach you through in this book.

There's a powerful way to learn complicated motor skills that isn't covered in the traditional methods of coaching. This way embraces the power of not only the body but also of the mind, to make full use of the powerful biological system that is the human being. It allows us to flow our way into the zone of peak performance, enabling us to learn and excel as athletes, as well as in all areas of our lives. And this is the breakthrough process I'll be coaching you through in this book.

By covering nine different principles for improving and excelling as an athlete, we'll go on a learning journey of how to perform at the highest levels for your chosen sport. Through these potent principles, you'll gain a thorough understanding of the potential that we humans possess. And, as we develop your knowledge and skills, you'll learn how to trust in not only your own physical capabilities, but how to tap into the unlimited potential of our subconscious minds as you develop the ways and means to automate your motor movements, enter into the flow state, and get into the zone of peak performance in every practice, game, or competition. The best news is that these principles are universal and can be applied to any and every sport, whether played individually or as a team. They are also relevant to every sportsperson, whether they are a beginner or well on their way to reaching the level of a professional athlete. You have the power within you to achieve great things. Let me show you how.

Without further ado, let's dive right on into the way to become the pro athlete that both you and I know you are destined to be.

1

THE BIG PROBLEM

When it comes to learning the skills that are needed to become a pro at a sport or to take your game to the next level, there's a common problem that most people fall victim to. This misconception stems from the belief that meticulously and accurately defining the mechanics of a physical skill is the best way to learn it and reach higher levels of performance. This is the way that most of us are instructed when learning and improving a skill. But, as logical and reasonable as this approach may seem, it can cause much less progress than you expect, and far more headaches than you deserve. Let me tell you why.

The key flaw in this way of learning new skills comes from its 'mechanical' approach to defining how the human body works. We are not clunky contraptions of scrap metal and, as much like a supercomputer as our brains may be, they're not computers. In fact, our brains are far more powerful. Many studies done on skills acquisition have shown that the learning and performance process is far more automatic, if not natural, when we go in for athletic, physical movements rather than trying to understand the nuances, the ins and outs, of every move that we make. Our brains and nervous systems are incredibly resourceful. Rather than overwhelming them with analytical information, we should arm them with performance-based data, such as the way it *feels like,* or what we see, when doing the action we are trying to learn.

The optimum way to perform athletic actions is to do them as naturally and automatically as possible. This cannot be achieved if you are trying to over-analyze every movement that you make. When you reach the stage of being able to perform a skill or action 'automatically' in a sport, you're onto a winning formula and are then able to move confidently on to the next level of your performance. This should be one of your main goals of training and is often thought of as one of the defining characteristics of a true athlete. This is how I overcame the Big Problem of skills acquisition and became an expert in any sport that I set my body and mind to and it is how you can too.

In this chapter, we're going to go over the basics of how our bodies learn physical skills. Think of it as your introduction to the way that an athlete's brain (such as yours) works, and as your guide on how to evolve in any sport through the use of motor skill learning. Let's get you over the mechanical clunkiness of over-analyzing and onto the right path for successfully and efficiently refining your skills development process.

SKILLS ACQUISITION 101

When we think of improving our performance as an athlete, we're mainly talking about refining our motor skills. These are the skill sets that define our body's ability to complete certain actions and manage our movements to achieve specific goals. As we learn to perform better at skills such as running, weightlifting, perfecting that golf swing, or even just reaching for your cup of coffee, we are improving our control of the motor that is our body. This is what motor learning, or skills acquisition, is all about.

What is Motor Learning?

At its core, motor skill learning refers to the practice we go through to learn how to carry out actions or specific movements quicker and more accurately. To learn a motor skill, you need to practice it over and over again during many training sessions until you reach peak performance, or the plateau, for that skill. When we reach this stage, we should be able to now do that motor skill without having to focus on the movement or concentrate on the action. In other words, we'll be doing it automatically. As we'll get to in a little bit, this is the stage of performance you should aim to get to for every skill that you learn and practice. In other words, acquiring a motor skill is a combination of learning and experience.

- **Learning**

There are two ways that we learn motor skills. The first is known as the fast phase and deals with any skill that you can improve in quickly and effectively during a single training session. The second is known as the slow phase and is for skills that require a more gradual, steady improvement over many training sessions until you reach the performance plateau. Knowing whether you are practicing a motor skill that requires fast phase learning or slow phase learning is key to developing an effective training regiment, ensuring that you get the best bang for your training bucks or time, and making sure that you don't injure yourself in the process of learning it. It will also help you to keep motivated and not get downhearted at the small amount of progress made over a single or a couple of training sessions. This is especially true if you haven't worked your muscles or body in the way that this motor skill requires before, which is always going to be the most learning-intensive of practice sessions.

- **Experience**

In terms of practice, training, and experience, we can split skill acquisition into three stages. They are:

1. Encoding

This first stage of experience in motor skill development involves practicing the movements and actions to learn what they feel like and how your body needs to work. The encoding stage is often linked to the fast phase of learning, as you should see quite a bit of progress in your encoding sessions. As the name suggests, when we encode, we are aiming to experience what it's like to do the movements of the motor skill and to begin converting that experience into muscle memory, or at least storing the way that it feels in our brains for future reference.

2. Consolidating

After we've encoded the skill we're trying to learn, the next thing to do is to consolidate. Consolidation means that you bring things together into a single, more coherent, whole. In terms of skills acquisition, this means putting together the different movements you have encoded into a single motor skill, sometimes even combining different motor skills together to do so. This generally happens between your training sessions and is often a completely subconscious process. This is great news for you because it means that the best thing you can do for this stage of motor learning is relax, recover, or even sleep. When we are relaxing or sleeping, our brains aren't concentrating on a million different things or interpreting a bunch of sensory inputs so that we can continue to make sense of what's around us. This means that it's the perfect time for it to focus on consolidating what we have learned or practiced that day. In terms of the fast and slow learning phases, consolidation can be thought of as the space in-between them, or even as the glue that links them together.

3. Retaining and Recalling

The final stage of learning a motor skill is called retention. This stage is more closely linked with the slow learning phase and happens both during training sessions and during rest and recovery periods. It's during the retention stage that the skill you're busy learning makes its way from our brains and into our muscle memory so that you are able to recall that skill, action, or movement without consciously needing to think too much about it. This is the beginning of automating your motor skill learning. Armed with this knowledge, let's now move on to learning about the basics of how to acquire a new motor skill.

The Basics of Motor Learning

Our bodies are the vehicles through which we experience life, and motor skill learning is the way that we improve our control over this 'vehicle' to do specific tasks quicker and better than ever before. All it takes, at the end of the day, is practice. But there is a lot more that goes into skills acquisition and improving your motor skills than just turning up day after day. You want better results than just a participation award, after all! So, let's go over some of the basics that you'll need to understand about motor learning in order to acquire the skills you require like the pro athlete that you are or want to become.

- **Define Your Intention**

The first thing you'll want to focus on whenever learning a new skill is the reason why you want or need to learn it. What is your intention for acquiring this skill? How will it help you to improve your game and become a better athlete? Having a clearly defined intention for why you are learning this specific motor skill will not only help to keep you motivated come rain or shine but will also get the supercomputer that is your brain to back you, too. Our brains need to know the purpose for us doing something or understand our end goal in order for us to get the most help out of them. Not having your mind on your side when learning something new is like shooting yourself in the foot and then trying to run. Sure, you can do it, but you've severely handicapping yourself and it's going to be a whole lot more painful in a learning journey. This is why defining your intention is a vital part of motor learning.

• Work On Your Perception

After you know and have clearly defined your intent for the new skill that you're acquiring, the next basic of motor learning is to visualize your perception of it. We all know that it's almost impossible to be good at something new straight off the first try of learning or practicing it. And, even if we are good at it straight away, there's still a long way to go before we can call ourselves pro at it and automate that skill. It never helps, however, to have the mindset that we're crap at something. Negative thought spirals such as this are the antithesis of progress. We perceive what we believe and believe our perception of ourselves (and others) to be reality. In terms of skills acquisition, this means that we need to believe that we are capable of learning this motor skill and, using our intent, visualize what our end goal of learning it is. What will it feel like once we have leveled ourselves up with this new skill? What will we look like and how will it up our game? Once you've visualized your end goal, then look at where you are now in terms of acquiring this skill and then visualize your learning process that connects the present version of you to the one that's a pro at what you're trying to do. This is how to work on your perception and develop the mindset of a motor learning champion.

- **Calibrate the Actions**

After you've defined your intent and worked on your perception, the next step is to get to work practicing. This is where you take the motor learning journey out of your head and onto the playing field. You've already got the mindset and have a clear visual image of how the skill will feel and look once you've acquired it, now it's time to calibrate your body to reflect what you've got in mind. In this part of motor skill learning, repetition and reevaluation are the keys, with your aim being to practice and hone the skill until you can do it automatically (without thought) at the highest level. As UCLA basketball coach and player John Wooden once pointed out: "The importance of repetition until automaticity cannot be overstated." Take his advice to heart; he wasn't nicknamed the "Wizard of Westwood" for his skills on the field and later as a coach for nothing, you know.

The Stages of Motor Learning

With the basics of motor learning outlined, it's now time to move on to the three stages that we go through when learning a new skill. Although there are lots of different theories on what is the best way to learn a new motor skill, the most popular one was developed by Fitts and Posner way back in 1967. This not only makes it one of the most well-known models, but its continued popularity amongst sports scientists for such a long period of time means that it's definitely a goodie of golden advice.

Fitts and Posner's theory on the stages of motor skills learning and development deals with a continuum, ranging from when the most attention is required to learn the new skill to when the most practice time is needed to hone and develop it. Along this continuum, they have placed three different stages of learning. They are:

1. Cognitive
2. Associative
3. Autonomous

As we go through these three different stages, it's important to keep in mind that most athletes shift up and down the spectrum of attention and practice, sometimes on a daily basis or even in a single training session. Although we'd love to bring our A-game to every practice session, and it should definitely be our aim to try and do so, sometimes life gets in the way or we're just not feeling up to it on that day. This means that there will be days where you need to focus a bit more on doing the motor skill even though you'd auto-mated the skill and performed it without thinking for the entire last practice session. As such, it's best to think of the stages we're about to cover as 'fluid', with you being able to shift up and also down, the continuums of attention and practice. With that in mind, let's now dive into Fitts and Posner's three-stage model for learning a motor skill.

- **The Cognitive Stage**

In the first phase of the motor learning model, you're trying to figure out what exactly it is that you are learning to do. This is also known as the novice phase and involves working out what the requirements of the motor skill are, as well as understanding what the parameters of performing the action or doing the movement will be. The cognitive stage requires the most attention, as you need to concentrate hard on a number of different things, most of which will probably be new to you. Sometimes, it can be a bit overwhelming to take in and put into practice all of the information required, especially if you try to do it all at once. That's why it's a good idea to break any task into as many bite-size steps as possible, to make sure that you can digest it without succumbing to information overload. It's also important to remember that, although improvements are generally quite rapid at this stage and generally require less practice per gain than at later stages, you're going to be making a lot of mistakes. And this is okay! In fact, it's to be expected, even encouraged to a certain degree. As you learn how to problem-solve your way to success and try to get your mind and body to make sense of the motor skill you're learning, you will experience some obstacles and inconsistencies to overcome. It's all part of the learning journey, especially in the early days of learning something new.

- **The Associative Stage**

The next stage of motor learning is all about learning how to perform the skill and transforming the knowledge and understanding of what you need to do (the cognitive stage) into how to actually do it (the associative stage). This is also known as the intermediate stage of motor skill learning because it's the meeting point between attention required and practice time needed. Although you'll need to talk yourself through the steps of how to perform the motor skill a lot less than in the first stage, you still need to focus on thinking through the necessary steps and problem-solving your way to performing the movement as a whole.

The associative stage is also where you start to adapt the skill to you and your specific environment, taking in cues from the surrounding game aspect as to when is the best time to use the skill you are learning and what is the best way to perform it for success within the sport. Let's take an example from the world of tennis to see how it all works. Let's say that you're busy learning the motor skill of how to serve. In the cognitive stage, you would have had to begin by concentrating real hard on each and every movement or action required, self-talking your way through the different aspects of the serve to understand what the required actions should feel like and what your parameters of movement are. This would have included continuously asking yourself questions such as if you're holding the racket in the right way, if your feet are in the correct position at different times of the movement, how your arms should move and in what time order, and where you are aiming for, even if you don't get it quite there. As you move on from the cognitive stage to the associative stage, however, you'll begin to question your hand and feet positions a lot less as you become more comfortable with the placement and movements. Now, you can start focusing more on the external environment, such as where your opponent is standing on the other side of the net or how to time hitting the ball to develop the maximum amount of speed. In other words, you are now focused on joining together the way the action feels with your perception of how best to use it in a given situation. This is known as optimizing your movement or motor skill.

Timing the exact sequence of movements perfectly will still be a challenge at this stage, and many mistakes will still be made as you iron out the kinks. It's also important to note that your performance will vary greatly, especially if you try and compare yourself to someone who has already automated the movements. Don't forget that the associative stage is where practice and attention meet, so you'll still need to use your brain to work your way through the process. The intermediate level is where most people remain for a long period of time, if not forever. This is because most people believe that this is the end of their motor skill learning journey and that they can now stop investing so heavily in developing the skill. But, for us elite performers, that's not the end. True athletes have one more stage of motor learning to get to: automation.

- **The Autonomous Stage**

The final stage of motor learning is to develop the skill until you can pretty much automatically perform it with the minimum amount of thought possible. This means that the autonomous stage requires the most amount of practice time and the least amount of attention required. By now, you should be able to do the movements and actions almost effortlessly in terms of the conscious control needed to do them. This then allows you to focus more on reading and interpreting the cues from your environment, from your teammates, and from your opponents. To carry on with our tennis analogy above, this stage would involve observing where your opponent is standing on the court and then using this perceptual cue to inform you what the best serve would be, how much power you'd need to get it where you want it to go, and how much power to put behind the swing. Best of all, you don't have to work any of this out yourself, because you will automatically 'know' what the best course of action is.

Without needing to focus on controlling the action, your attention is freed up to think of what comes next, such as where you should move to after the serve in order to perfectly place yourself for the next shot. This is how you hone your skills for your chosen sport, take your gameplay to the next level, and become the athlete that you and I both know you can be.

One final word to the wise is that you shouldn't be scared of returning to the associative or even the cognitive stage to re-learn some key part of the motor skill, or to learn another action that can be combined with the skill to further improve your gameplay. Nothing in sport is ever just a "one-and-done" and there are always more combinations of motor skills to practice into automation in order to take your performance to a higher level. In the next chapter, we'll carry on with our work on how to reach the hallowed grounds of automaticity by learning about how to turn your autopilot on and embrace the power of the subconscious to become the best performing athlete you could dream of being.

2

TURN AUTOPILOT ON

One of the main things that separate a pro athlete from a run-of-the-mill sports player is that the pros not only use their muscles and lungs but also their minds. And not just using their conscious minds, either. When performing a motor skill, we often think that it has to be a conscious effort to do so. But this is not exactly true. In fact, controlling complex motor skills has more to do with the subconscious than with the conscious mind. This is because it's in our subconscious where most of the immense power of our brains is located. While our conscious minds may struggle with how we can do a task or achieve a goal, our subconscious minds are focused on doing whatever it takes to achieve a specific goal. Believe it or not, our conscious minds can actually hinder and handicap our subconscious by trying to over-analyze the movements and actions needed to learn or perform a specific motor skill.

In this chapter, we'll learn more about the massive power of the subconscious and how you can make full use of it to learn any motor skill and achieve your athletic goals. After that, we'll take your automaticity knowledge to the next level as we cover the three *Fs* of motor skill automation—fluency, fluidity, and flexibility. Finally, we'll end off with a chat about going with the flow and the importance of letting go of self-control in order to up your game. Let's get you on the right track to becoming the pro athlete that leaves everyone else eating their dust in terms of your ability to learn and perform motor skills. And it all starts with trusting the supercomputer autopilot that is your subconscious.

THE SUBCONSCIOUS ATHLETE

Let's begin this section with a little illustration of the difference between the way that our subconscious and conscious minds work. When our brain has a specific intention or action in mind, it visualizes this motor skill as a whole before moving any single body part or flexing a muscle. This means that, before you make that serve or swing that golf club, your subconscious has already created a complete model of the motor skill movement you're about to make. Your brain then directs your body to complete the model it's formed, without you even consciously thinking about the fact that you have already visualized a model of the action.

This is why our conscious minds aren't nearly as capable of handling high-level skills and actions, because they get in the way of this visualized model of what to do by trying to think about it too much. As we covered in the previous chapter, we should only try and consciously work out every step and every move of the skill when we are in the cognitive stage of motor learning. This is because we first need to teach our subconscious the movements and actions of the motor skill and provide it with a model to work with. But this is only when we are beginning to learn the action or sport. As we advance toward becoming a pro athlete, we should leave behind the awkward, slow, self-conscious stage of skill development that is the conscious and automate our way toward attaining peak performance by relying on our subconscious minds.

The Conscious vs. the Subconscious Mind

As we have seen, our conscious minds might be the place where all of us start out when learning to play a sport or add a new motor skill to our repertoire, but we should aim to move away from it toward automaticity as quickly as possible. We have a very limited scope when it comes to what we can consciously focus on, with most people only able to think about or do a small number of different things at a single time. Not only that, but our conscious minds take a long time and a lot of energy to take in and interpret the information we need to make sense of the situation and our environment. The final shortfall of the conscious mind is that it's often occupied with negative or self-defeating thoughts that weaken our resolve and distract us from performing at peak performance.

On the other hand, the subconscious mind is able to focus on a large number of actions and movements at a single time once they have been automated. Because the job of our subconscious mind is to store, retrieve, and interpret environmental information in the blink of an eye, it is able to absorb and adapt to situations with a lot less energy and way more speed than our conscious minds can. Finally, the subconscious mind doesn't care about our debilitating, self-defeating negativity; it just does the action based on the info it's got without needing to reason through why it's doing so and how well it is executing it. That is why pro athletes learn to rely more on their subconscious minds and automaticity when pursuing peak performance rather than their conscious minds and over-attention.

Getting in the Zone

If you combine the power of your subconscious mind with the natural talent that you have for a specific sport, you're on a winning path to competitive success, no matter the level of the competition. As all athletes know, it's important to get yourself in "the zone" when practicing or competing in any sport. This means reaching a state of complete focus, zoning into the game, and forgetting about everything else in order to reach peak performance. To reach this state, also known as the "flow state" (more on this in a little bit), you're going to need to let your subconscious mind take the wheel of the motor vehicle that is your body. This doesn't mean completely disconnecting your conscious mind, though, as you'll need that to focus on the intricacies of the game and to recognize the different moves and movements that your opponent makes or elements that the environment throws at you. In other words, to get fully in the zone, your subconscious mind needs to become the driver and your conscious mind the navigator. Collaborating together, they synchronize the actions of your body and improve your reaction times to respond to what's happening on the game field in the best way possible.

• Overthinking Leads to Underperforming

If you want to reach the zone of peak performance, you're going to need to learn how to manipulate your overthinking, self-controlling conscious mind into letting your subconscious take the wheel. As the famous tennis player and three-time Grand Slam winner Arthur Ashe continuously pointed out, if we rely on our conscious minds while playing sport, we'll end up in "paralysis by analysis."

The bottom line is that enforcing complete self-control is not the aim of pro athletes, and, as such, it should not be your aim, either. This is because over-thinking or overanalyzing not only slows down your reaction time during the game but can also negatively affect your motor skills while learning a skill and hinder your coordination when practicing it. In a recent study carried out at Nottingham Trent University, sports scientists confirmed their suspicions that athletes who overthink, overanalyze, and try to exert too much self-control over their actions, both before and during competitions, performed worse in terms of the fluidity of their motor skill movements. Those who didn't try to control or think through every aspect of their game found it much easier to reach a state of flow or get in the zone and performed their motor skill movements at a more fluid and improved level. In other words, think less, feel more, and play better.

ENTERING THE FLOW STATE

So, what exactly is this state of flow that gets you in the zone of peak performance? If you ask athletes that have achieved it, like me, we'll all tell you a pretty similar thing. It's the feeling of being invincible; of being so involved in your chosen sport that the rest of the world seems to fade away. Your point of view zooms in to completely revolve around the moment, the movement, and the play of the game. But few are those that can call upon the flow state on the regular or predict when it will occur. In this section, I'll arm you with all the tips and tricks you need to know to become one of them.

The Dimensions of Flow

The term "flow" was first used by psychologist Mihaly Csikszentmihalyi back in the 1970s. He was researching the reason why some artists and painters became so focused on the work they were undertaking, so involved in their present artistic endeavor, that they would often forget to drink, eat, or even sleep. After his initial research into the state of flow in artists, Csikszentmihalyi quickly realized that the concept could be expanded into the world of sports. In 1999, he wrote a book along with the two-time British national champion of figure skating, Susan Jackson, titled *Flow in Sports: The Keys to Optimal Experiences and Performances.* This book and Csikszentmihalyi's theory have defined the nine dimensions that sports psychologists use to train athletes in the ways of achieving the state of flow to this day. The more of these dimensions that you can incorporate into your gameplay, the more likely you'll be to reach a state of flow and enter the zone of peak performance. With the background info out of the way, let's now dive into the nine dimensions of flow and how to use them to take your performance to the next level.

1. Challenge-Skill Balance

The first of the nine dimensions of flow deals with finding your ideal balance between the skills you have and the challenges you face when practicing your chosen sport. As an athlete, you're going to be challenging yourself to reach higher and higher levels of performance as you become less of a beginner and more of a pro, but you don't want to feel like you can't overcome a challenge you set for yourself or are incapable of completing the task. If this happens, then your conscious mind will kick in with a lot of negative feedback about how you're just not good enough, bring up memories of that time when your dad or coach (from some unfortunate people, it's both in one) told you that you'll never amount to anything or any other experience that highlights your flaws. As soon as this spiral of negativity and judgment kicks in, it's nigh on impossible to get into a state of flow. So, to stop this from happening and increase your chances of reaching the hallowed grounds of the flow state, you'll want to make the challenges you set yourself to be just out of your reach, but still achievable at a stretch. And if you need to overcome a challenge that you seem to be incapable of overcoming with your present skill set, then break this task down into smaller milestones that are achievable with a stretch.

2. Action-Awareness Merging

The second dimension of flow is about becoming one with the activity you are performing or the sport you are competing in. This might seem a bit zen, but, then again, zen is exactly the mindset that you need to have if you're to consistently enter into the flow state, my friend. Merging your action and your awareness comes when you feel like you are one with your performance. Through this merger, you will become so absorbed in the movements and actions that your awareness will be completely consumed by the activity and your focus limited to the task you are presently performing. You will become harmoniously engaged in your sport. From this emerges a sense of peace and prosperity and of belonging to and in the moment that is key to achieving automaticity and getting in the zone. If you can automate this merging of action and awareness, then you'll be onto a winner of a formula for entering the flow state on the regular.

3. Clear Goals

While the flow state may be about reaching a stage of zen and oneness with your sport, that doesn't mean you don't need to have clearly defined goals in order to enter it. It's not all about letting go of self-control, but also about clarity of purpose and intent. To remain completely focused on your purpose when performing a sport is not an easy thing, and you'll find that it fluctuates on an almost moment-by-moment basis. We are bombarded by distractions in the modern age and these distractions won't go away as soon as you step onto the sports field. Unless you make them, that is. To enter into the flow state, you need to remain focused on your specific goal and fully connected to the task at hand (such as perfecting a motor movement or winning a game). You need to have a clearly defined goal in mind and know exactly how to accomplish it.

4. Unambiguous Feedback

As we mentioned in the point above about action-awareness merging, you need to become one with the activity you are performing. This means remaining responsive to your internal body and your external environment and using the cues that they give you to process your performance. This is where clear and unambiguous feedback comes into play. The word 'unambiguous' means something that is not open to multiple interpretations. In other words, your conscious mind shouldn't be able to twist and turn the feedback you receive into its own interpretation, as this will take you out of the moment and ruin your flow. But receiving feedback is essential to improving your performance, especially when given while you are performing. Whether you receive this feedback from your coach, your parents, your partner, or your own body, you should make sure that you are open to receiving it by viewing the feedback as objectively as possible. Furthermore, make sure that the feedback is simple to interpret and that you can process it quickly without too much conscious thought so you can take it in your stride and tweak your performance accordingly. If you think that someone is giving you complicated or unneeded feedback (such as your dad on the sidelines), then make sure to tell them to either simplify their message or keep it for after the game, because they are stopping you from entering your flow state and reaching peak performance.

5. Total Concentration

Along with clearly defining your goal and being responsive to unambiguous feedback, you also need to hone your concentration until you can totally focus on the task at hand. Being completely present and focused on a task is one of the best ways to tell if you're in a state of flow or not because the flow state is engaged from being centered in and focused on the present moment.

6. Sense of Control

This focus on the present moment is also what is needed for the next dimension of flow—to have a sense of control over what you are doing. When you reach the stage of total concentration and have merged your action and awareness to become fully connected to the sport you are currently engaging in, you'll begin to develop a sense of owning the moment; of being in control and confident about what you are doing. This feeling will empower you and free you from one of the biggest adversaries of the flow state: fear of failure. It's not that you won't fail at times, even the best of us do. But through developing a sense of control, you'll change your perspective of what failure is, viewing it more as a lesson or as vital feedback rather than a debilitating shortcoming. By disconnecting your negative thoughts and worries about failure, you'll become even more capable of reaching the flow state and overcoming the challenges you need to overcome if you are to reach the next level of your performance. Remember that your success or failure depends on you, not on some external element.

7. Loss of Self-consciousness

This next dimension of flow carries on with the idea that we need to let go of our debilitating or negative thoughts. These thoughts stop us from making mistakes or from trying something new just because we may fail at it or not be as good as others are at it. This is why entering the flow state needs to come more from the subconscious rather than the conscious mind; our consciousness is just too concerned about what others think about us. As a social species, we humans are naturally going to compare ourselves to other people around us and evaluate our success compared to theirs. But, this constant need for comparison and evaluation prevents you from focusing fully on your actions and movement and therefore hinders you from flowing your way into the zone of peak performance. That's why you should aim to automate your motor skills as quickly as possible and develop the flow dimension of total concentration as thoroughly as you can. Remember to keep comparisons off of the sports field and to focus on achieving total concentration for the present moment. Slowly but surely, you'll feel your self (consciousness) fall away in favor of the grander game of the flow state.

8. Time Transformation

As we spoke about earlier in this chapter, one of Csik-szentmihalyi's main reasons for beginning his research into the flow state was to discover why some artists seemed capable of losing all sense of time, becoming so immersed in their work that they went extended periods without eating, drinking, or even sleeping. This, he discovered, was because the sense of time for those in the flow state becomes distorted. On a moment-by-moment basis, it may seem like time has slowed down. But, when looking at the clock at the end of the game, it may feel like it's passed in the blink of an eye. This is another clear tell that you have entered the hallowed grounds of the flow state and comes about due to you totally concentrating on your actions and the activity and letting go of your sense of self in favor of focusing on the game. With your actions and awareness merged in this way, time itself falls to the wayside, transformed to help you stay in the flow state.

9. Autotelic Experience

The final dimension of flow is known as the autotelic experience. In a nutshell, this means that your reasons for performing a task or playing your sport should be for internal gratification, not external rewards. This should come about as a result of combining together as many of the other eight dimensions of flow as you can. The word autotelic comes from two Greek words that, when combined, mean doing something for its own reason, or for its own purpose. This makes the state of flow more about the journey than about the destination, which means that you should aim to enjoy the experience more than the end result.

Congratulations! You now have a clearly defined way of thinking about flow and how to understand the state of mind and being needed to reach it. In the next section, we'll work on some activities that you can use to help you get your flow on and reach the zone of peak performance.

Condition Yourself to Flow into the Zone

Now that you know about the definition of flow and its dimensions, it's time to teach you how to reach this hallowed ground and get you into the zone so often that you can automate the experience. Using Csikszentmihalyi's groundbreaking research once more, as well as tried-and-tested methods of sports psychologists, we're going to go through seven different activities that you can put into practice today to start inducing the flow state in your sports practice and games. And, don't stop there! The flow state can be expanded to every aspect of your life. Once you have incorporated the following tips and tricks into your training regiment, you'll find it easier and easier to automate the feeling of flow until you can call on it to get in the zone for anything and everything you do. Ready? Set. Let's go!

1. Focus on Your Body

Have you ever noticed how doing exercise makes you feel *damn* good? As an athlete, I'm sure that you have. But, did you know that it's not only those happy chemicals called endorphins that help our minds feel positive after a good run or sesh at the gym? Our bodies also just plain love a good workout. To help you get into the flow state, focus on this joy that you feel in both body and mind when exercising, training, or playing a game.

Become aware of the skillful machine that is your body and own your physical prowess. Develop the skill of finding pleasure in honing your body and you'll find that you become far less self-conscious and far more likely to enter into the flow state on the regular.

2. Calm Your Mind

As every human on the planet knows, our minds are generally places of disorder bordering on chaos. We have so many thoughts running around, emotions bouncing up and down, and half-baked plans pulling our attention in every direction that it's a wonder we as a species are able to get into the flow state at all. But, we are and you can. All you need to do is learn to calm your mind, leave the outside world off of the field, and concentrate on the game. Easier said than done, I know. But if you're to flow into the zone of peak performance, you're going to need to learn how to calm your mind. To achieve this, meditation is your best friend. Sit down in a quiet and comfortable place, close your eyes, and focus on your breathing while trying to keep your mind blank. Make this a daily habit, internalize the feeling, and automate the breathing procedure. If you develop a meditation practice, you'll soon find that all you need to do is to take a few deep breaths before a practice or game to calm your mind and introduce the meditative flow state into your sports performance.

3. Use Memory to Your Advantage

Just like taking a few deep breaths will help to calm your mind by entering you into a meditative state, remembering positive experiences or past successes will help instill in you the confidence needed to shirk off self-doubts and reach peak performance. When you recall a time you achieved a goal or overcame some challenge, you start to feel the positive emotions that you felt at that time. Just like negative memories can make us feel sad or bad, positive memories can make us feel happy and good. Leverage your memories to your advantage, focus on the bright side of life, and watch your ability to flow into the zone bloom and flourish.

4. Streamline Your Thoughts

When we become "lost in thought", time itself seems to change, with the moment seeming to last a lifetime but passing in no time at all. This weird feeling of time dilation is also the same when we enter into the flow state. To get into the zone of peak performance, you're going to want to streamline your thoughts so that you don't end up getting lost in the chaos of daily life while on the field. Consciously focus your thoughts on your breathing, on your body, and on the movements of the game, and avoid distractions at all costs. If you find yourself getting easily distracted, then isolate the distractions and work out ways to remove them from your sports time. Streamline your thoughts until the only 'thought' that you get lost in is the flow state.

5. Communicate Positively with Yourself and Others

As social creatures, we humans seek out ways to interact and communicate with other people. It helps us to develop connections, both mental and social, and to reach insights that we might not have been able to reach on our own. Even if talking to others isn't your favorite thing to do, it's still vitally important to help develop your thoughts and discuss ways to problem-solve your path to victory. Two brains are better than one, after all! Communicating with other people is also one of the keys to achieving unambiguous feedback, especially if it's a coach or fellow athlete providing the feedback to you. Besides talking with other people, it's also important to develop a healthy way of communicating with yourself. Through self-talk, we define the way that we think about and react to certain experiences and situations. Negative self-talk is also one of the biggest killers of the flow state. To flow like a pro, you're going to want to develop positive self-talk, as well as to surround yourself with support capable of providing you with unambiguous feedback communicated in a way that you can use to improve without feeling self-conscious about it.

6. Embrace the Idea of Lifelong Learning

One of the most helpful mindsets you can develop to aid in flowing into the zone of peak performance is that of being a lifelong learner. If you develop this kind of mindset, then you'll begin to better understand your skills and limitations, become more open to the feedback that you get, and be more connected to the experience of training, playing, and performing your sport to the best of your ability. This is a key part of obtaining the flow dimension of the challenge-skills balance.

Use these six tips along with your understanding of the nine different dimensions of flow to get into your zone and reach ever higher levels of performance. There's one more piece of useful info that I can give you on how to reach the much sought-after flow state, and that's to make use of what we call the triggers of flow. One more section and you'll be armed with everything that you need to know to get into the zone on the regular!

The Triggers of Flow

While the dimensions of flow and the tips for optimally conditioning yourself to enter it come directly from Csikszentmihalyi's own research, the four triggers of flow we're about to cover come from later research conducted by New York Times-bestselling author and executive director of the Flow Research Collective, Steven Kotler. In his groundbreaking book *Rise of Superman*, Kotler expands on the groundwork laid out by Csikszentmihalyi and suggests that there are specific exercises we can do to bring on, or trigger, the flow state. Kotler holds that we can only flow into the zone of peak performance when we are completely focused on the present and that we should seek out exercises to increase our ability to keep our attention at the moment. Without further ado, let's jump into the four categories of flow state triggers.

1. Social Triggers

Although we've been talking about entering the flow state to achieve individual gains, it's also important (and pretty interesting) to note that it's possible to get into the flow zone with your team or in a group. Also known as collective or group flow, this state is achieved through continuous practice with one another and a "meeting of the minds". It results in more effective and productive gameplay, higher levels of performance, and increased capabilities of the team as a whole. The social triggers that bring this about focus on the flow dimensions of challenge-skills balance and clear goals, as well as unambiguous feedback and total concentration. Added to these dimensions are the elements of familiarity amongst team members and compatible skill levels within the team.

Another thing that can serve as a social trigger of the flow state in a team or group is cohesion. When we play sports with other people and have a shared goal, each player merges their needs and aims into the cohesive whole we know as a team playing to win. In the best teams, there aren't individual egos vying for the top spot in the team hierarchy, but rather a blending of egos that, while keeping their sense of control, work smoothly and equally together as one body. This is collective flow.

There are certain exercises or practices that you could incorporate into your team or group training in order to reach the collective flow state. Let's go over a few of them quickly:

- Make sure that communication between team members is positive and encouraging in order to increase unity and camaraderie.

- Practice together to increase familiarity and confidence in your skills as a team.
- Don't be afraid to take calculated risks that stretch the team's abilities to their limit; overcoming such challenges is a great team builder.
- Focus on team goals over individual goals, and make sure that everyone in the team is aware of what is expected of them.
- Speak up when you feel the need to raise an issue or air an idea, but also listen and engage when your team members do the same.

2. Creative Triggers

The second category of flow triggers we're going to cover deals with the creative spirit within us all. The kind of creativity we're talking about here has nothing to do with your artistic flair, so don't worry if you can't rhyme to save your life or if your drawing skills peaked at stickmen. If you are to reach peak performance in your sport, you still need to think creatively, just in a different way to what an artist would need. Every person has their own creative way of approaching a problem, realizing an opportunity, or presenting an idea. Not only can you use your creative way of solving problems or recognizing patterns to improve your likelihood of flowing into the zone, but the flow state also heightens your creative gameplay. This makes the creative triggers we're about to cover an excellent example of a positive feedback loop for the athlete. Flow into the zone with the use of the following creative triggers:

- Use your imagination when approaching a challenge. Try to think outside of the box and take a variety of angles to each problem you have to deal with.
- Be a goal-setter and a goal-getter. Believe in yourself and your ability to constantly improve. Once you achieve one goal, use it to raise the bar of your performance and to set the next!
- Embrace the thrill of taking calculated risks, and trust in yourself in being able to overcome them. To tackle a challenge or problem head-on and overcome it successfully is one powerful thing and will help you to develop the confidence needed to reach the next level of your performance. And, if at first you don't succeed, remember that you are a lifelong learner and you have just gained some invaluable feedback on how to improve before taking a new angle and trying again.

- Step outside of your comfort zone and experience something new, something unfamiliar. Through doing this, you'll not only become more confident but will also learn to see things from a different perspective and be able to use these new experiences to come up with solutions to problems that you wouldn't previously have thought of. The flow state is about getting into the zone of peak performance, not about remaining in your comfort zone.

3. Environmental Triggers

As we athletes know, there are rewards that come from taking calculated risks, from pushing our boundaries, and from stepping out from our comfort zone in pursuit of better and better performance. It goes with the turf of competitive sports to move the mark of what we are capable of as far forward as we can and it's part of the environmental trigger of the flow state to embrace this kind of mindset (just remember to keep your challenge-skills balance in mind too). It's important to know that, while it takes routine to reach the stage of productivity and automaticity required to start entering the flow state, you should always be looking for ways to up your game in order to further increase your ability to enter it on the regular. Remaining with the same routine in the same environment day after day is not the way to flow into the zone of peak performance; it's just another comfort zone. Let's look at some exercises you can use to develop the experiences and environment needed to activate this next trigger of the flow state:

- Develop a rich training environment and a deep level of embodiment with whatever environment that you find yourself in. This means that your training environment (or environments) should challenge and push you to do better and that you should learn to adapt to a wide variety of different training experiences and environments. Never be a big fish in a little pond, always seek out bigger and better ponds to train in. Figuring out the unpredictable is a more useful way of becoming one with the moment than knowing the predictable.
- Do things that are personally meaningful to you. Seek out environments, activities, and experiences that will help you to grow emotionally, intellectually, or socially. If you find yourself getting into a rut with your chosen sport, try something else that you have

always considered to be holding you back from being the person that you want to be and work toward achieving it. This could give you the different perspective that you need to break through your rut and get your groove back in your sport.

- Go for a walk in nature. This might seem like a weird one, but it is highly helpful in getting in touch with the mindset required to flow into the zone. Hiking or walking in nature encourages you to connect with your environment, focus on your body, and get in touch with its movements. You can then take this heightened physical awareness and use it to flow into a training session.

4. Psychological Triggers

The final trigger of the flow state is to make use of psychological cues that allow you to increase your ability to focus on, and concentrate in, the moment. As we learned about in the dimensions of flow section, the flow state needs you to hone your focus to the point of total concentration through having clearly defined goals, amongst other things. You also need to receive unambiguous, sometimes immediate, feedback and to achieve a balance between your skillset and the challenges that you set yourself. These are all examples of psychological triggers for getting rid of distractions or other impeding factors that could stop you from flowing into the zone of your peak performance. Let's have a look at some of the exercises you can do to activate these psychological triggers:

- Write down your personal goals according to your current skill level. Reevaluate these goals as your skills improve and celebrate every time you achieve one. This will help your mind to cement down exactly what you want to achieve and to tell your brain that it feels great to work toward and achieve these goals.
- Make a mission statement for yourself by completing the following phrase: "I want to achieve X by Y because it will help me to achieve Z."
- Learn to rely on your own personal validation for things. It may feel good to have people cheering your name, but this shouldn't be the way that you legitimize your success. Rather focus on the goals you have set for yourself and your own path to achieving them rather than relying on external validation or worse constantly comparing yourself to others.

And, there you have it! The way to turn your autopilot on and flow into the zone of your very own peak performance. Remember that automating your motor skills and entering the flow state for your sport doesn't mean remaining in your comfort zone. In fact, it's the opposite. In order to reach the flow zone on the regular, you're going to want to continuously challenge yourself according to your new and improved skills. This is how you reach the level of the pros. In the next chapter, we'll carry on with what it feels like when you reach the level of a pro athlete and how you can feel your way there too. Let's go!

3

DO YOU FEEL LIKE I DO?

I f you had to ask almost any professional athlete to describe their approach to performing at the highest level possible, they'd all tell you the same thing: play by feel. We don't think in terms of individual body parts, and we don't consciously control our movements to form actions. If we did, human beings would be some of the clumsiest creatures out there. It's impossible to mechanically think our way through an athletic motion. And, as we saw in the previous two chapters, it shouldn't be our aim to try and do so. In fact, it should be pretty much the opposite.

To perform your sport at the highest level possible, and to consistently and reliably do so, you're going to need to heighten and refine your senses until you can *feel* your sport. In this chapter, we'll be talking about something called proprioception—our perception and awareness of our body positions and movements in relation to our surroundings as we exercise or play our sport. We'll start by defining what exactly proprioception is all about before going over some tools, tips, and exercise techniques that you can use to improve your perception and awareness of your body today. After that, we'll move on to how practice really does make perfect as we cover the true benefits that showing up day after day has on the brain of the professional athlete. Time to take your performance to the next level!

PROPRIOCEPTION: AN ATHLETE'S SIXTH SENSE

If you observe a pro athlete at the top of their game, you'll notice that not only are their muscles and movements primed for peak performance but their ability to take in and interpret sensory info is also heightened. This is because athletes hone their bodies and their senses to perform at ever higher levels. With their sight, they are able to rapidly track the movement of the ball, of team members and opponents, or of the terrain itself in the blink of an eye. With their ears, they can hear the approach of an opponent, even over the screams and cheers of the crowd. With a touch of their fingers, they can put a different spin on a ball specifically tailored for what they feel is needed at that time. They can smell the change in weather, taste that sweet victory, and...you get the picture. But pro athletes have also developed and honed a sixth sense—that of proprioception.

As I mentioned in the intro to this chapter, proprioception refers to our ability to sense our body positions and to predict the best movement to make for a certain situation. It comes about by training the nerves in your muscles to send more detailed info to the brain about how much speed, force, and pressure you should apply to complete the activity or overcome the challenge you are currently facing. Your brain then uses this feedback to work out how hard it should flex certain muscles, how much your joints have to bend, and how large of a next step you should take. And, like we don't have to understand the nuances of the eye or the ins and outs of the ear to see or hear, we don't have to know how the brain does this to make use of proprioception. Let me give you a simple example of how proprioception works.

I want you to close your eyes and point your index finger up in the air. Can you still sense where it is? You can't see, feel, hear, taste, or touch it at this moment, but still know where it is located in relation to your body and the space surrounding it. Now, twirl that index finger of yours around, eyes still closed. Once again, you can still tell what it's doing without using any of the other senses. This is proprioception at work. Obviously, the motor movements we require in sports are a lot more complicated and way more strenuous than just twirling a finger around. As such, it's important that athletes hone their body's ability to know its own movements and the space that it has to do those movements in.

Our Proprioceptors

Just like our eyes receive and monitor light signals to the brain, our receptor nerves, or proprioceptors, send signals between the brain and our muscles, joints, and ligaments. Our senses send information to the brain, which then sends messages to our muscles telling them what they need to do. At times, this happens so quickly that it's not even considered a reaction, but rather a reflex. There are certain key components of proprioception for you to know about if you're to start honing them reactions and quickening those reflexes. Let's now go over the proprioceptors that move and groove you into the zone of peak performance:

- **Kinesthetic Awareness**

Although kinesthetics isn't exactly a proprioceptor, it's so closely linked with proprioception that they are often considered one and the same. Kinesthetics is about the way that we use body motion and our perception of it together to perform our motor skills to the best of our abilities. This makes it pretty similar to what proprioception is, but there is a key difference. Where kinesthetic awareness is the conscious way that we react to situations and the bodily effort we put into dealing with them, proprioception is the subconscious or even unconscious way that we do this. This means that proprioception can be considered the end goal of some kinds of kinesthetic awareness because you'll have automated your reactions and movements to the degree that your brain and body will be acting as one. This is achieved through continuous practice and perseverance.

However, most of the time, we use kinesthetic awareness and proprioception together to perform the necessary motor skills needed to play your sport smoothly and efficiently. Let's use an example from skiing to show you what it's all about. A skier will use proprioception to keep balanced and vertical while they ski. They don't need to think about this, but rather do it subconsciously. At the same time, though, a skier is consciously processing what they need to do to maneuver around trees or how to tweak their hands in a way that adjusts their bodies and skis to make it over the next slope. This is kinesthetic awareness at work. In this way, kinesthetic awareness is the external sense of our bodies and proprioception is the internal sense of the nervous system. You need to train both to be in perfect sync to become a pro athlete.

- **Golgi Tendon Organs**

Found in-between a muscle and its tendon, the Golgi tendon organs (GTOs) are the sensory receptors responsible for sensing and providing information about changes in muscle tension. When we flex or contract a muscle, our GTOs are activated. As we change the amount of strain we put on our muscles, these proprioceptors provide info to the brain to help the muscle in question perform the required action. If there is too much tension or force put on the muscle, then the GTO will stop it from becoming injured through over-exertion. As soon as your GTOs sense an imminent overload of tension, they'll send warning signals to your brain to stop you from injuring yourself. That's why it's important as a pro athlete to keep your GTOs in top shape. To do this is pretty easy. You just need to stretch it out regularly, especially before doing exercise. When you hold a low-force stretch (one that isn't too strenuous or painful) for more than seven seconds, you'll activate your GTO as it tries to reduce the tension in your muscles. This will allow you to deepen your stretch and safely increase the range of motion that you have in your muscles to further improve your motor movements. So, learn a set of static stretches that affect the muscles you need for your sport, hold them for 7-10 seconds, and do this before (and after) you practice or compete to make sure that your body movements are primed for reaching peak performance.

- **Muscle Spindles**

The next proprioceptor for you to know about in order to take your performance to the next level is muscle spindles. These are small sensory organs that are wrapped around our muscles. As a muscle lengthens or stretches, the spindle also stretches. The spindle signals the brain when your muscle has contracted to the limit and protects you from overstretching it. This is known as the stretch reflex. When you stretch a muscle spindle rapidly, two things happen. First, the muscle spindle signals the muscle to contract in order to stop it from stretching too far too early on in the stretch required to do the motor movement. Second, it stops the opposite muscle to the one you are currently stretching (known as the antagonist muscle) from contracting to stop you from over-stretching. This is called reciprocal inhibition. Once more, stretching is your friend when it comes to improving your body awareness and getting a feel for how your muscle spindles work, as well as what the antagonist muscles to the ones you need for your specific muscles are. A great stretching habit to develop would be that of yoga. Yoga is a great way to develop your body awareness, hone your muscles, decrease your chances of injury, and increase your chances of reaching ever higher levels of peak performance.

Exercises for Enhancing Proprioception

There are a number of different exercises that you can do to train and enhance your sixth sense of proprioception. Before we get into them, though, it's important to understand that both sensory and perceptual systems are used when performing a motor function. Our sensory systems are to do with sight, smell, hearing, taste, and touch, while our perceptual systems are those that make use of our senses to interpret the world around us. Our primary perceptual systems are visual, auditory, and kinesthetic for interpreting pictures, sounds, and feelings. These are the three perceptual systems that you'll need to focus on enhancing to reach the next level of your performance. Besides static stretching and doing yoga, there are other exercises that you can do to increase your proprioception, improve your body awareness, and better link your sensory and perceptual systems together. Let's arm you with a few more!

- **Balance Exercises**

Balance exercises are great for developing your proprioception because they improve your ability to control the position of your body and to equalize your body weight while doing different motor movements. Almost any activity that you do when moving your two legs will help you to maintain a good balance. But, if you're to reach peak performance, you need to go beyond good balance to excellent balance. One tool that you can use to improve your balance is a balance board, which can be bought from most sports equipment shops or websites. Other than that, let's go over some of the main balance exercises for you to introduce into your training:

1. Weight Shifts

A good starting place for improving your balance is to practice weight shifts. Begin with your feet hip-width apart and your weight spread out equally across both legs. Then, shift your weight onto one side while lifting your other leg off the ground. Hold this position for around 30 seconds to start with, or for as long as you can keep good form. Keeping good form means keeping your muscles tensed and not swaying or moving. After this, return to the beginning position and repeat the same with the other leg. Increase the number of sets that you do as you gradually improve your balance.

2. Single-Leg Balancing

After you can comfortably hold the weight shift for 30 seconds or more in good form, then move on to the single-leg balance. Start in the same position as the weight shift exercise, but this time with your hands on your hips. Then, lift your one leg off the ground and bend your knee backward while keeping your other leg straight on the ground. Once again, aim for 30 seconds or as long as you can hold it while keeping good form and increase the time as you improve. Then get back into the starting position and repeat it with your other leg. Increase the number of times you do this as you improve. Once you've got it down with your leg bent at the knee backward, then it's time to upgrade the motion. While standing on one leg, move the leg that's in the air from having your knee bent backward to stretching your leg as far forward as possible without letting it touch the ground. Once you've perfected doing this motion for 30 seconds in multiple repetitions, then it's time to move it up a notch once more. Do this by standing on a pillow or some other type of unstable surface while doing the same single-leg balancing exercise.

3. Bicep-Curl Balancing

This exercise combines the use of dumbbells with the balancing exercises we've looked at above. Begin in the usual position as the other two balancing exercises, but this time with a dumbbell in your one hand. Hold the dumbbell with your palm facing upwards and then lift your opposite leg, bending your knee backward. Aim for 30 seconds, or as long as you can hold it without swaying or moving and while tensing the muscles of the leg on the ground. Then, return to the starting position before repeating with the other leg and your dumbbell in your opposite arm, palm facing upward. Increase your repetitions as you improve. Once you can do it comfortably with your knee bent backward, then practice it while moving from knee bent backward to leg stretched out forward. Once again, to increase the difficulty, stand on a pillow or some other kind of unstable surface. You can also hold the dumbbell in the same hand as the leg you have lifted off of the ground (right hand and right leg, for example).

- **Eyes Wide Shut**

After you've practiced honing your proprioception using the three balance exercises covered above, try and perfect doing these same activities with your eyes closed. By completing exercises with your eyes closed, you enhance the communication channels between your brain and your muscles. This will result in you developing more than just your balance. By practicing with your eyes closed, you improve the trust you have in your muscles so that you can work on performing motor skills without needing to watch the movements that you make. Once you have gotten this skill down for the balancing exercises above, then branch out and practice other motor skills for your sport with your eyes closed.

- **Exercises to Strengthen Your Body**

In order to improve your proprioception, you need to not only enhance the communication channels between your brain and your muscles, thus increasing your body awareness and motor skill control, but you also need to connect the muscle fibers themselves to work better together. This is achieved through increasing your strength. As an athlete, you'll know that you need your body to be in prime shape and strength if you're to compete at the highest level you can. Besides the training that you do to improve your motor skills, this is the other cornerstone of every athlete's training routine. And strength building is not only done for the body, either. As you increase the strength of your muscles, your brain will develop the habit of accepting your request for more and more strength, forcing the proprioceptors to allow your muscles to lift more and for longer before they start to give the warning signals of possible injury. This allows you to perform a motor skill or hold a movement or action in place for a longer amount of time in the proper form of peak performance. While strength training exercises very much depend on the sport, and you should research what is recommended to increase muscle strength for yours, there are a few general exercises you can introduce into your training routine to begin increasing your strength today. Here are some exercises for establishing the connection between your muscle fibers:

1. Knee-Strengthening Exercises

The first category of strength-building exercises for improving your proprioception has to do with the knee. Knee problems are a worry for many athletes across a wide variety of sports, especially those that have to do with running in some way or form. In fact, according to bestselling health author and former USA Olympic team medical advisor Dr. Josh Axe, knee pain or problems account for around one-third of doctor visits to do with muscle or bone pain in the leg. That's why every athlete worth their salt and intent on staying in the game long-term should introduce knee-strengthening exercises into their training routine. Let's go over some common knee-strengthening exercises for you to include:

a. Squats

Begin by standing in a position with your feet placed hip-distance apart and your butt slightly pointed out. Make sure that all of your weight is placed on your heels rather than on your toes and then act like you are sitting down on a chair, sticking your butt back further and further while keeping your upper body as straight as possible. When you reach the limit of where your thighs are still parallel to the ground, hold this position for a couple of seconds before returning to the starting position. Aim for around 10-20 repetitions of squatting it out.

b. Single-Leg Squats

Once you have practiced and perfected the double-leg squat, it's time to take your knee-strengthening game to the next level. As always, begin with your weight distributed evenly, feet hip distance apart and your weight focused on your heels. Then, transfer all of your weight onto your one leg, using the other leg to keep you balanced by touching the ground with your toes. You should also focus on something stationary in front of you to help remain balanced. When you have spent a few seconds getting used to this position, sit back on your grounded leg, keeping your weight on your heel, while raising the other one and extending it in front of you. Push that ass back and go down as low as possible in the same sitting-down–in-a-chair motion. Once again, keep your back as straight as possible. Then, return to the starting position and do the other leg, aiming for around 10 repetitions on each side.

c. Step-Ups

The next knee-strengthening exercise is called the step-up. And, as the name implies, you're going to want to find something you can step up onto, such as the first or second stair or a fitness bench at your gym. Just make sure that whatever you choose to step up on is not going to budge as you do so. Assume the position of feet hip distance apart, weight distributed evenly. Step onto the stair or bench with your one foot before following it with the other. Then, step back down in the same foot order. Change up which foot steps up and down first so that you start with the opposite one every time, and aim for at least 20 repetitions of this movement. It might seem simple, but it helps to increase your knee strength to no end and prepares you for the next two exercises we're going to look at.

d. Step-Back Lunges

Assume the position once again, this time making sure that you're standing in a place with lots of space behind you. Then, take a step backward with your one leg and bend your knee down to the ground. Make sure that you don't extend your knee below your ankle and to keep your upper body as straight as possible. Then, push off the ground with the heel of your backwards extended foot to return to the starting position before repeating the same movement with the other leg. Aim for around 10 repetitions for each leg.

e. Step-Forward Lunges

The final knee-strengthening exercise that we're going to look at is the step forward or front stepping lunge. Assume the starting position, this time making sure that you have lots of space in front of you. Step forward with your favored leg and lunge down, once again making sure not to extend your knee beyond your ankle. Also make sure to keep your weight located in your heel to get the most out of your muscles, and your upper body nice and erect. Once you've lunged all the way down, push off with the heel of your extended leg and return to the starting position before putting the other leg through the same movement. Aim for around 10 repetitions for each leg.

2. Lat-Strengthening Exercises

The next kind of general exercises that every athlete should include in their training regimen are those that strengthen the latissimus dorsi muscles, a.k.a., the lats. The lats are one of the largest muscle groups to be found on the human body. Located on our backs, they are responsible for lifting up our arms, doing shoulder extensions, are involved in rotating our torsos, and providing support and stability for our core strength. If you aren't activating and strengthening your lats during training, then at best your arm and spine movements won't be primed for peak performance. At worst, you'll end up injured or suffer from chronic shoulder pain or lower back pain. Let's have a look at some exercises and stretches that you can do to increase your lats:

a. Lat Pulldowns

Lat pulldowns are a great way to improve the strength of not just your latissimus dorsi muscles, but also your shoulders and your core. If you have a gym member-ship, then you can use a lat pulldown machine. Choose if you want to sit down on the bench of the machine or kneel on it with one or both of your knees, depending on the position that allows you to grip the bar evenly above your head. Pull the bar down to your chest while making sure that your back is kept straight before raising it in a controlled way back to the starting posi-tion. Do between 10 and 15 repetitions in a set, two or three times a week, followed by a stretch or two after to keep your muscles nice and limber.

If you don't have a gym membership, it's not a problem. You just need to go out and get yourself a resistance band from your local sports shop. They're pretty cheap, but invaluable for increasing your proprioceptive strength. Begin by putting the band around a high point that is stable and won't fall down no matter how much you pull on it. Then, grab each end of your resistance band while keeping your arms straight in front of your head. Then, bend your elbows to pull your hands as close to the front of your chest as you can manage. Do this in slow, steady, and controlled motions, aiming for 10–15 repetitions two or three times a week. Follow it up with a couple of stretches once again to ensure you keep your ultimate levels of flexibility.

b. Pull-Ups and Chin-Ups

Another great exercise tool for working on your lats is to get yourself a pull-up bar or to use one at your local gym. Face the bar and grab it with your palms facing toward you and your arms extended. Then, lift and pull yourself up, keeping your torso as straight as you can. Try and lift yourself up until your head is level with or above the bar before slowly lowering yourself back into the starting position. After that, take a breath before repeating the move, doing about 5–10 repetitions.

c. Seated Rows or Dumbbell One-Arm Rows

If you want to increase your shoulder, back, lat, and core strength, then you should include rowing into your exercise routine once or twice a week. Not everyone has the luxury of having a large body of water to row on or a boat to row with or hire, but everyone can include rowing in their exercise routine. All you need is a gym membership or some dumbbells. Every gym worth its salt will have a rowing machine or three. Sit yourself down at one of them with your knees bent, your shoulders in line with the handles, and your back straight. Then, grip the handle with both hands and pull it toward you, bending your elbows and pulling your shoulder blades together as you do so. Breathe in as you pull it toward you and out as you go back to the starting position. Aim for around 30 minutes on the rowing machine per session.

If a gym membership is beyond your budget at the moment, no worries. You can use dumbbells and a bench in place of the machine. Grab a dumbbell in one hand and put your opposite knee and palm on the bench. Make sure that the arm on the bench is kept straight and your torso flat. Then, lift the dumbbell to the side of your chest and bend your elbow. Keep your stomach muscles taught, movements slow, and strength controlled. Then, return to the starting position, making sure to move slowly once again so that it's not momentum or gravity that brings the dumbbell back down but your strength. Aim for 10–15 repetitions before moving to the other side of the bench and repeating the procedure with your other arm.

d. Trunk Lifts and the Held Squats

The next two lat strengthening exercises are the laying trunk lifts, also known as 'Supermans', and the held squat, a.k.a., the yoga chair pose. For the Supermans, start by lying down on the ground with your fingers joined together behind your head. Then, lift your shoulders up to engage your back muscles. If you're struggling to keep your feet anchored in one place, try lifting your toes a bit. If it's still a struggle, then try putting your feet under something to keep them stationary, like a bar or a bed, or have someone hold your ankles still. Raise yourself until most of your lower back is off the ground, making sure to breathe steadily. Also make sure to move slowly, and not to jerk your neck or overextend it. Do between 5–10 repetitions per set, increasing the number of sets you do as you improve.

As for the yoga chair pose, begin with your feet close enough together that your big toes are touching. Then, raise your arms straight above your head with your palms touching one another. After that, all it takes is to imagine that you're sitting back in a chair. Bend those knees of yours, stick that ass out, and sit down in your imaginary chair. Make sure to keep your arm at full extension and your back as straight as you can manage while breathing shallowly and steadily. Maintain this position for between 5 and 10 breaths, trying to breathe deeper with every inhale.

e. Lat Stretches

The final category that we're going to cover for strengthening your latissimus dorsi and improving your proprioception is the stretches you need to do to keep your lats in prime condition for peak performance. Lats are pretty easy to stretch because all that you need to do is to raise your hands above your head and extend them fully. This is called the standing overhead reach and is a great way to stretch out them lats during your post-workout cool-down. Bending slightly from side to side is a good way to increase this stretch, but make sure to still keep your back straight and not to jerk or yank. Slow and steady is the way. Hold the standing overhead reach for 10–30 seconds.

The next lat stretch for you to use is called the kneeling arm stretch. It's pretty similar to the standing overhead reach, except that this time you'll be kneeling and won't be reaching for the sky, but will be stretching your hands out, palms together, with your face facing the floor. Reach your arms out until your fingertips touch the floor as far in front of you as you can reach so that you fully engage both your shoulders and back muscles. Hold this position for 10–30 seconds while taking deep breaths so that you soften your muscles. Mix it up by either lifting your hips up or keeping them down at your heels. Also mix up lifting your chest and tailbone and keeping them down to the ground so that you can stretch your back in multiple directions. Once more, slow and steady winds, while yanking around or moving too quickly could result in doing more harm than good.

And there you have it, folks. We've come to the end of this section on the athlete's sixth sense of proprioception. Now you know what it's all about and the different exercises to include in your training to hone those proprioceptors, it's time to put it into practice. And, that's exactly what we're going to be covering in the next section—the importance of practice in making and molding the pro athlete.

PRACTICE MAKES BEST

There are two choices in life. You can either do your homework and own your progress or you can find excuses to tell yourself and others for not doing it. There are no in-betweens when it comes to reaching peak performance, or...not. To play with the pros and reach the highest levels of skill in your sport, we need to put in the needed practice time and do it with both intent and accurate feedback. Much of this feedback is gained through the use of your senses. Use your touch, sight, and sound to increase the awareness you have of your body movements and muscle contractions, as well as of the ball, the bat, racket, or club. And don't forget about the athlete's sixth sense of proprioception that we covered above!

Through rigorous training, a stone-cold drive, and sensational feedback, you will improve and refine the sophisticated biological system that is the human body. As your practice hours rack up, you'll start to feel like time itself slows down while you're performing your sport and your motions and motor skills themselves will seem to become way simpler to perform. This is the power of showing up, doing your homework, and making sure that you're doing the right kind of practice at the intensity of a pro. Ultimately, this practice and work will form the basis of your ability to rely on yourself no matter what situation is thrown at you or what kind of pressure you are under. It's only with this kind of preparation that you'll start to possess the power to perform your motor movements automatically and reach your peak levels of performance when it matters.

Having done all of the work beforehand, your inner self, also known as your subconscious, will have what it needs to succeed. If you stop putting in the effort, though, you won't have what you need to come out on top. Through practice and preparation, you'll not only develop the body to deal with the stress of competing at the highest of levels, but the mindset to do so too. In this section, we're going to go over how exactly it is that practice changes the brain of an athlete, as well as the importance of developing the habit of being a life-long learner if you're to play with the pros and stay doing so.

Mold Your Mind Through Consistent Practice

I'm sure you've heard the saying before "It's like riding a bike" when talking about how, once we've learned some kind of motor skill, we never forget how to do it. And, believe it or not, this is pretty much true. If we learn a complex motor skill as a kid such as riding a bicycle, rock climbing, or even ice skating, we are likely to be able to call on that muscle memory and brain synapse anywhere from the ages of 6 to 60. However, this doesn't mean that we're going to be very good at it or be able to compete with the pros. Not straight away, at least. Your brain might remember how to do the motor skill motions, but if your body is not primed for them or your muscles haven't been used in that way for a long time, you're going to struggle to keep up with other players.

The fact that we don't forget a motor skill that we learn is due to a property of the brain called neuroplasticity and is a good thing for those of you who are looking to pick up your chosen sport again after a lengthy hiatus of not performing it—you can do it! Especially if you went through rigorous motor skill training and practice when you did play and compete in that sport. In a nutshell, neuroplasticity refers to our brain's ability to change its own structure as we learn through forming and reorganizing its synaptic connections. These synaptic connections form and reorganize in response to the things that we learn and experiences that we have and can even reform back into old neural pathways after we've recovered from injury, helping us get back into peak performance after a bout of sickness or an unfortunate accident (within reason, of course).

If you go through intensive motor skill training, it's not only your muscles that will noticeably change, but your brain itself will physically change too. This is measurable using an fMRI machine and has been recorded by various neuro researchers studying the cerebellum (the part of our brains responsible for coordinating and regulating our muscular activity). Up until pretty recently, most studies carried out on how our brains control our movements focused on how some diseases seemed to impair our motor skills. But, more recently, neuro researchers have become interested in what it is that allows the pros to perform better at a wide variety of physical skills (some even outside of their sporting expertise) when compared to the rookie.

One such study was carried out by the Department of Medicine at Imperial College London. It compared a dozen black belt karate pros with an average of 14 years experience in their sport with a dozen regular Joes who, while exercising regularly, didn't have any specific background training in karate. Led by Dr. Ed Roberts, the study tested the punching skills of these two test groups. The karate punch is more than just a strength-packed hit; it involves coordinating speed, strength, and wrist motion with shoulder and torso movement, making it quite a complicated motor skill to learn. While it's obvious that the black belts' punches were way more powerful, the researchers made an interesting discovery when they studied the cerebellum of the two groups. The pros' brains were significantly different in terms of the structure of their white matter when compared to those of the amateurs. This advanced structure of their cerebellum allowed the black belts to repeatedly punch with a level of skill and coordination that a beginner just couldn't produce, no matter how much natural talent or skill as an athlete they may have had.

So, what does this mean for you? Well, it means that all of those hours you devote to training your skills and honing your body really do pay off. More than just your body, though, all that practice also reshapes and rebuilds the architecture of your brain, programming motor skills that will last a lifetime and ensuring that you reach your ultimate potential for your chosen sport. Practice is how you become one lean, mean, supreme performing machine.

A common notion in sports performance is that we want to perform a motion or motor movement with robotic-like consistency and accuracy. This makes it a compliment to say that someone played like a 'machine'. But, it's important to keep in mind that we humans are not just machines. In fact, we are way better because we have the ability to adapt. Let's take the seemingly repetitive motions of swinging a bat, a golf club, or even a hammer or ax. The brainwave patterns for such motor movements differ each and every time. They don't just duplicate over and over again. And this is a good thing! It tells us that our brains are making numerous subtle adjustments during the action as they adjust hundreds of muscles and thousands of nerve connections to make the perfect move for the present situation, circumstance, or environment. This once again proves that we need to let our subconscious minds be in control. We can't possibly control all of those functions of our brain and body with only our conscious minds; it would be like trying to verbally give all of the instructions in a matter of one or two seconds. In the next chapter, we'll dive more into how our subconscious works to run the sophisticated mind-body system that is the human being. Let's get going with the next step in your journey to reaching peak performance!

4

TRUST ME, I KNOW WHAT I'M DOING

I f you want to reach the heights of peak athletic performance reserved for the pros, then you're going to need to truly trust in your biological system and its ability to perform at the highest levels. This is the essence of our power to adapt, improve, and excel; a power that is potentially tremendous, defying any definition that mere words could provide. However, if this potential is stifled by disbelief or handicapped by our self-criticizing conscious minds, it will never be able to reach the peaks of ultimate athletic performance. So far in this book, we've gone over the ways to automate your motor skills and methods for flowing into the zone of peak performance, as well as some exercises for getting more in touch with your bodily awareness. This has all been to provide you with the understanding and techniques you'll need to access and utilize the true potential of the human athlete.

We can accomplish more and achieve higher levels of sporting success when we learn to trust in our own potential. Our mind will learn, process, and allow us to perform better than we could even fathom if we just let it. In this chapter, we'll go into more detail as to the true power of the subconscious mind for an athlete and how to focus your attention on reaching peak performance. It's time to embrace the power of your subconscious and learn how to use it to ensure that you reach your full potential.

THE POWER OF PAYING ATTENTION

In order to become a pro athlete performing at the highest of levels, you need to do more than just show up and spend time practicing. You also need to pay attention while doing so. This is called attentional focus and, in terms of playing sport or doing exercise, refers to "the process in which the athlete allocates mental resources to cues, stimuli, or states" (Neumann, 2019). This means that, although the subconscious reigns supreme when it comes to reaching peak performance in sports, we can't just let our conscious minds wander freely and expect the subconscious to do the work it needs to. As we saw when we spoke about getting into the zone in Chapter 2, we need to focus our attention on the moment and the movement, linking our action and awareness, if we are to reach the hallowed grounds of the flow state.

Practicing the skill of paying attention is the way that we consciously link together our sophisticated mind-body systems with the subconscious. It doesn't mean that we control either the mind or the body while it's performing the action (it's overtly impossible to command these systems to do things), but that we place our attention wholly on the task at hand, hone our focus and bodily awareness, and then completely trust and believe that our subconscious knows what it's doing and how to do what we ask it to.

Attentional Focus

There are a few different dimensions of attentional focus for you to know about if you're to hone your focus to the highest of levels. Some of these dimensions are more relevant to some sports rather than others, but it's still good to know about what options you have out there so that you can choose and use the ones most relevant to you. Attentional focus is best understood through the dimensions of direction and task relevance. The first dimension of attention has to do with the direction in which you place your focus, and it can either be internal or external. The next dimension of attention has to do with the relevance of the task that you're doing and how to view it. This dimension is split into association (living an experience with feeling) or dissociation (viewing the experience as if from a distance).

Through using a combination of these different dimensions, we get the following categories:

1. Internal Association

Internal association takes into account factors like muscle fatigue, the changes to our breathing when we do different kinds of exercises, and any pain we suffer from accidents or injuries.

2. Internal Dissociation

The second category of attentional focus deals with things like daydreams, problem-solving, and memory recall.

3. External Association

External associations are the ways that we monitor and keep track of our progress and goals. This means that this next category is about things like recording split times, placing distance markers, or setting your targets.

4. External Dissociation

The final category of attentional focus is about environmental factors like the scenery that surrounds you, social factors like the crowd and all the distractions or encouragement that comes along with it, and audio factors such as listening to music.

The Benefits of an External Focus

Now that we've covered the dimensions and categories of attentional focus, it's time to go over which ones you should focus on for reaching peak performance, and which ones you should try and reduce the influence of. Research conducted on attentional focus strategies for sports has shown that external focus is better for reaching peak performance than internal focus. This is because, when we focus our attention away from the body and instead focus on motor movement, we are better able to learn and more capable of reaching superior levels of performance. Focusing your attention on the body doesn't necessarily impair your actions or movements, but it doesn't let you go above and beyond what you are capable of, or to flow into the zone of peak performance. In other words, an external focus benefits our progress and performance, whereas an internal focus merely allows us to perform.

Some of the benefits of developing your ability to focus externally, especially for motor skill learning, including improving the effectiveness of your movements, such as in improving your proprioception and balance, as well as ensuring increased levels of accuracy for the motor skills you are learning and performing.

An external focus also increases the efficiency of your movements, streamlining your muscle actions, heightening the levels of your peak performance, allowing you to perform your motor skills at greater speeds, and increasing your endurance so that you can perform at peak levels for longer periods of time. Besides increasing the effectiveness and efficiency of your movements, an external focus also improves the form of your motor skills, allowing you to better automate your actions and making your movements more fluid than if you focused internally on the body.

As you can see, developing the right kind of attentional focus is key for honing them motor movements and shaving off those few extra seconds on the clock that mark the difference between the skilled amateur and the pro. Develop an external focus away from the body and on the movement itself, allowing your subconscious to take control of directing the body while you focus on your goals for performing the movement itself. Let's go over an example of how this works.

Let's say that you're a baseball pitcher working on perfecting your throw. To improve your pitch, you need to focus on the motion that your arm makes, as well as the movements of your body as you make the throw. Focus your attention on the motor skill, merging your action and awareness, and reflect on your technique afterward to provide yourself with the unambiguous feedback that your subconscious can use to improve for next time. This feedback could go something like this:

"I feel like I was too fast with my arm and wrist throwing action, which made me throw to one side and miss my target. How can I correct this? Let me review my body motions by focusing my attention on my arm and wrist actions for the next few throws, trusting my subconscious to correct the miss in my throw through feeling and observing what my body does. Now that I've analyzed it some more, I see that it's actually my legs that were moving too fast. Let me try adjusting the speed of swinging my legs as I make the pitch...bingo! I hit my target. Now, time to practice until I can automate this improved motion. Then, onto the next step of becoming the peak-performing pro I know I am."

The above example gives you a taste of how having an external attentional focus and tying it in with an unambiguous feedback loop can help you to improve your motor movements to the point of peak performance. Now, to take your knowledge to the next level.

GOAL-ORIENTED THINKING

When we pitch a ball or swing a tennis racquet, golf club, or baseball bat, we don't focus on the ball or the racket. In fact, it's better if you don't focus on hitting the ball. We should instead place our attention on the target, on our goal. Having goal-oriented thoughts of what we're trying to do, not how we're going to do it, is the key to reaching peak performance. Focus on your intended target and trust in your subconscious to hit the ball on the exact trajectory or direction required to reach it.

Our minds and bodies do way better when we focus on achieving the real goal. If you solely focus on "hitting the ball", you won't get the result you're looking for. You're much more likely to get a pop fly for baseball, an out-wide shot in tennis, or a shanked ball in golf. In these cases, you *did* hit the ball, but with all of the wrong results. Rather, focus on the goal of a line drive hit to left center, an arcing tennis shot down the sideline, or a stinging low bullet golf shot in the center of the fairway. If we give our subconscious the focused goal of what we want to achieve and then allow it to control our body and motor movements to achieve it, we will become far more capable of reaching peak performance. Accomplish this, and your mind and body will do whatever it takes to make your goal happen. In this section, we'll go over some ways that you can become a goal-getter, set your targets, and hit them every time.

Goal Setting for Athletes

As I'm sure you've picked up by now, if you didn't realize it already, setting goals is one of the most important things that you can do to ensure your success as an athlete. More than that, though, goal-setting is the key to living a successful and rewarding life. Setting goals allows us to easily evaluate our progress and to make changes to our targets at exactly the right time to ensure we reach the next level of performance, as soon as possible. Through creating and monitoring your goals and targets, you'll be setting up your own unambiguous feedback loops that provide you with all the info and motivation you need to flow into the zone of peak performance, whether it be in a practice session or in a competition. And, they don't all have to be long-term goals, either.

As we covered in the section above, focusing on your goal or target for a specific motor movement is far more beneficial than trying to control what it is your body is doing during that movement. You are far more likely to hit your target if you focus on it rather than on "hitting the ball". Make sure that your goals are specifically focused on improving your performance and evaluate them frequently as you progress. A little word of caution before we carry on, though, is to never confuse goals with expectations. What do I mean by this? Well, simply that while you should set goals that are challenging and push you to improve, you shouldn't force strict and stringent expectations on yourself. It's healthy to set goals, to work toward achieving them, and to evaluate them often while keeping in mind that goals can, will, and should change. It's unhealthy to weigh yourself down with lofty expectations, such as anything that follows the phrase: "I *have* to...".

When we give ourselves the ultimatum of an expectation such as having to make the next 10 shots in a row, we set ourselves up with a win/lose scenario that sets you up for either complete victory or complete failure. And, more often than not, if you do make the next 10 shots, you'll probably push the goal post by saying that now you have to make the next 10 too. If you don't meet your expectations, even if you somehow managed to make the first 10, you begin to question your ability. This disconnects the subconscious and reconnects the self-deprecating conscious mind, severely reducing your chances of flowing into the zone of peak performance. You are setting yourself up to fail before you've even begun if you focus on expectations rather than on your goals. With that out of the way, let's now go over the ways that you can set yourself up for success by creating goals that enhance your ability to reach peak performance.

- **Think SMART**

The SMART structure is one that is used in almost any profession where goal setting is necessary. If you want to compete at the same level as the pros, then you're going to want to plan and achieve your goals using this goal-setting strategy. It will help you to get rid of all guesswork and generalities when it comes to defining your goals, as well as provide you with a refined time-line that will make it so much easier to track and monitor your progress. Finally, this model will help you notice when you reach the next level of your performance or identify any milestone that you may have missed along the way. SMART stands for:

1. Specific:

Define your goal as specifically as you can. To do this, I suggest you answer the questions: What is it that you want to achieve (what is your target)? Why do you want to achieve this? Who do you need, or who can help you, to achieve your goal? Where and when is the prime place to practice? How will you go about reaching your goal (what will you need to get or do)? An example of a specific goal is something like: "Improve my percentage of free throws made." Another would be: "Increase the number of tackles I win during a 90-minute soccer match."

2. Measurable

After you have specified what it is that you want to achieve, the next thing to do is to quantify that goal. This means working out the measurable milestones that show you when you've reached the next step in your progress, as well as telling you when you've achieved that specific goal. It's vital that you keep track of your progress and know how far you've still got to go before reaching the finish line of achieving your goal. Examples of measurable goals are: "Improve the percentage of free throws I make from 25% to 40%," or "Win over 90% of the tackles I make during a 90-minute soccer match for the rest of the season."

3. Achievable

Once you've specified your goals and worked out your measurable milestones for achieving them, the next step is to make sure that these goals are, in fact, achievable. You don't want to set yourself up for failure by placing your expectations so high that you can't actually achieve the goal you've set yourself. You want to be realistic, albeit with a stretch. Take your goal and determine if it is actually achievable with your current skill set if you 'stretch' those abilities of yours to their limit. If it is, great! If it isn't, reevaluate your goal. You can always update to the next level once you've achieved it at the realistic-with-stretch one. Examples of achievable goals are: "Improve the percentage of free throws I make from 25% to 35%," or "Win 80% to 90% of tackles I make during a 90-minute soccer match."

4. Relevant

The next step in setting your goals the SMART way is to make sure that they are completely relevant to improving your performance. To do this, you need to work out why this goal or target matters to you, and how it will help you on your overall journey of becoming the best athlete you could possibly be. And don't use external factors such as becoming better than other players in your team, when defining the relevance of your goal. It should be of personal relevance to you in becoming the best sportsperson that you can be or helping your team to secure a win. This step of the goal-setting model is where you decide on your reason, or motivation, for achieving your objective and is essential if you're to show up day after day, come rain or shine. An example of relevant goals would be: "I'm improving my free throw because it is one of the main deciding factors in a game and will benefit me in helping my team secure the win." Another is: "The more challenges I win and the more successful tackles I make, the better my team's defensive capabilities will be and the fewer opportunities our opponents will have to score."

5. Time-Based

The final step of setting smart goals is to make sure that they are time-based and time-bound. This means that you should set deadlines or a timeframe for accomplishing your objective and reaching your target. Remember that this timeframe that you set needs to adhere to the other parts of the SMART model. In other words, the time period to achieve your goal needs to be specific, measurable, achievable, and realistic. If you are working on a large goal or objective, try and split it up into smaller steps or periods of time to make sure that you keep yourself as time-based as possible. The trick to creating and accomplishing great goals is to not let them stretch out to infinity and beyond, but to contain them within a certain achievable timeframe that gives your subconscious mind a deadline to work with. Otherwise, there's no pressure to reach the next tier of your performance and, as such, you'll probably never reach that lofty peak of becoming a pro athlete. Examples of time-bound goals are: "Improve the percentage of free throws I make from 25% to 35% within the next 90 days," or "Win 80% to 90% of tackles I make during a 90-minute soccer match for the rest of the season."

With that, we have come to the end of this section on how to become an unstoppable force of a goal-getting athlete, and to the end of this chapter. Remember to place your attentional focus on external motor movements and to have SMARTly defined goals, and you're onto a winner of a formula for arming your subconscious with everything that it needs to succeed in the smallest level of individual movements and the largest level of achieving your overall goals, objectives, and targets. You'll need both ends of this spectrum if you're to become the peak-performing pro athlete that we both know you deserve to be. Now, onto the next chapter where we'll dive deeper into the world of motor movements in terms of its explicit and implicit learning components. Onwards and upwards!

5

OBSERVE, DEAR WATSON

As we have seen so far in this book, one of the key principles to learning a physical skill is to practice observation and awareness while letting your subconscious do the work of actually performing the motor movement. Through this, we gain the unambiguous feedback that we need to not only improve but to succeed. By implementing the process that I've outlined in this book, you'll become much more effective in refining and modifying your skill sets while making it feel almost effortless as you flow into the zone of mind ideal for reaching peak performance. By merging your action and your awareness, focusing your attention on the external movements rather than the internal bodily processes, you'll develop the ability to *feel* your actions as an extension of your body while you perform and/or practice. This will allow you to tap into the powerful self-correcting instincts of the subconscious. If we have SMART targets and accurate intentions while we practice and perform, we will instinctively improve. Over time, you'll begin to strengthen the habit of continuous improvement and develop these neural pathways to the stage where acquiring and perfecting new skills comes as naturally to us as walking and talking.

In this chapter, we're going to carry on learning about how to naturalize the motor skill learning process through developing the right kind of observational awareness. We'll take your automatization knowledge to the next level by defining the difference between implicit and explicit learning before finally covering how to refine your skills to ever higher levels of performance. We are nearing the peak of the pros, so carry on reading and let me teach you how to reach the height of your athletic capabilities. As Sherlock Holmes would say, "It's elementary, my dear Watson."

DON'T MAKE IT HAPPEN, LET IT HAPPEN

When we observe ourselves or others, we humans have a natural response of trying to give constructive criticism that almost always goes too far. We end up chastising, swearing, or unfairly judging ourselves as we try and control each and every element of our performance to more and more frustrating results. This is a massive obstacle that most people need to overcome when learning or improving a physical skill. If you try to make this learning process happen rather than letting it happen organically, you will come up against the obstacles of tension and stress, or even the brick wall of losing faith in yourself or trust in your abilities. But this is only the case for those who aren't armed with the knowledge of how to correctly observe their movements, and how to use the unambiguous feedback they get to mentally and physically rehearse their way to improve. Let's give you an example from the world of golf.

Let's say that you're working on your golf swing. By placing your attentional focus on the external factor of your motor movements, you've observed that you're pulling shots too far to the left of your target. For the next few swings, you test your hypothesis as you do the same actions while picturing and observing the motion of your arms and club as they direct toward the target in the distance. Then, physically rehearse the correct movement in slow motion once or twice, focusing your attention internally on the feeling of your muscles from toes to feet, legs to fingers, and hands to arms to torso. Mentally rehearse yourself hitting the ball to your target, this time focusing on the motions as you return your attention to motor movement. Finally, let go of making the shot happen, focus on your external target, and ask your subconscious to follow through with achieving your goal. After that, all that's left is to take the swing, observe your progress, and repeat. This way, you never over-control your actions, but allow and trust yourself to perform them in the desired way.

If you focus on the observation as you perform the action, you'll naturally process the feedback that you get. For example, let's say that, after going through the process outlined above, you feel that you now have a slight delay in your left forearm and wrist when making your swing. This was a natural adjustment that resulted from your goal of not pulling your shots to the left. Rather than getting frustrated or stressed out at this, though, just reprocess it as being the next step on your journey to improving your swing; as your next mental and physical rehearsal to go through. Then, visualize and take the next shot. As we said earlier on in this book, practice does indeed make perfect, as well as helping to strengthen those neural pathways and hone them for peak performance.

This is a breakthrough process that naturally taps into the most powerful subconscious regions of your brain. The process becomes finalized as you refine the high-level motor skill to the point that it becomes automatic for you to perform. As you can see, it all comes down to how much you know about the way that motor skills work, and how well you can get your subconscious and conscious minds to work on the tasks they are most suited for. After that, it's just a case of observe, feedback, rehearse, and repeat.

MOTOR SKILLS REVISITED

In Chapter 1, we went through a brief introduction to motor learning, breaking it down according to the three stages of motor learning (cognitive, associative, and autonomous). Now, we're going to add to that knowledge of yours a bit more as we learn about a little something called implicit and explicit motor learning. The idea of being able to streamline and enhance the process of learning a motor skill is one that should excite each and every athlete out there. It sure does excite me, and I'm sure that it does send shivers of possibility down your spine too.

Explicit vs. Implicit Motor Learning

Traditionally, coaching handbooks and sports psychology have focused on the explicit way of learning a motor skill through instruction-based models, methods, and modules. In the traditional way, it was assumed that athletes learn motor skills by first going through a "verbal-cognitive phase." This means that a coach or other sports player first needs to talk the athlete through the motor skill that they'll be learning, providing them info and rules about the technical side of the action and the facts about the way to execute the movement. This was thought to improve performance by having a more experienced player preach down the experiential knowledge that they had learned like a mentor to an apprentice. Then would come the practice and routine procedures that took place until the young athlete had memorized and automated the motor skill to the point that they were now barely conscious of the movements they were making.

Nowadays, though, sports such as baseball, soccer, and even football, prefer to adopt the newfound alternative of *implicit* motor skill learning. In the implicit motor skill learning method, you don't start with the verbal breakdown of facts and rules, but rather by directly gathering the procedures required for the motor movement through practicing it. This knowledge of the procedures can't be gained consciously and doesn't rely on the active memory of the athlete. Instead, it focuses on activating the subconscious which, as we have seen so far in this book, is the true powerhouse of automating motor skills and of reaching peak performance. This also means that the young athlete doesn't have to rely on someone being able to explain the motor movement to them, but on them being able to *feel* it. Most people aren't the best at explaining things and, if pressed to verbally describe the nuances of a technical motor movement, most players and many coaches will end their attempt with something along the lines of "you've just got to *feel* it." The implicit method of motor learning skips past the verbal break-down which, let's face it, often confuses us or bores us to no end, and focuses instead on this final statement. To learn a motor skill, you just have to learn how to feel it. This way, you're focusing on automating your motor control and reducing your conscious mind in favor of your subconscious from the get-go.

Just like nothing happens in isolation, no sport is performed in isolation either. There is always a multi-tude of different situations at play. From monitoring your opponent's movements to observing the surrounding environment, to balancing out the most rewarding next move with the risk of getting injured from doing it. And, of course, there's always the stress that builds up from competing at high levels, or the fatigue and psychological strain from giving it your all.

All of these dual conditions occur in almost every game that you play and you don't want to be conscious of them while you've got your game face on or else you'll never be able to reach peak performance. That's why the pros focus on letting go, letting their subconscious minds take the wheel, observing the results, and improving through unambiguous feedback after the fact. This is what implicit motor learning is all about, and why it's a better choice for athletes and their aim to automate their movements in order to deal with the dual-task conditions of the sporting world.

6

THE SECRET OF BALANCE

Humans have survived as a species for millions of years. We've accomplished this even though we don't have claws or fangs, or even a lot of fur to protect us from the other creatures out there or from our natural environment. How have we done this? Well, we are one of, if not the most, adaptable species on the planet. We have continuously changed, strategized, and refined our tools, actions, and techniques all in the name of survival. And, due to the laws of survival of the fittest, it is the most adaptable, strong, and quick-thinking of our species that have propagated and passed on their genes to the next generation.

One aspect of our evolution that is of particular importance to athletes has led to one of the most phenomenal skills that we possess. This is the skill of balance. Our ability to balance while standing on two legs has enhanced our capacity to develop and refine aspects of our movement and has allowed us to perform a vast number of skills that would have been impossible to do without it. Without our highly evolved sense of balance, almost all of the most popular sports of the modern day would be impossible to play. In this chapter, we're going to stretch and grow your knowledge on balance and coordination, providing you with insights into what makes us humans so special and why we are born to be peak-performing athletes, as well as how to use these skills to reach the next level of your own performance.

BALANCE AND COORDINATION

Being able to balance is an ability that has carried us *homo sapiens* from cavemen to the upright men and women of the modern day. It is a survival mechanism that we've passed down through the generations, with those of our ancestors who couldn't maintain their balance while doing an activity falling, getting injured or eaten, and most probably dying before they could pass on their inferior genes. Which is a good thing! Because it means that we have ended up with the highly advanced sense of balance that we enjoy today. But, although this is easy to describe, describing how a person maintains their balance is extremely complicated, if not impossible. It's something that we subconsciously do, not something that we have to consciously think about.

Let's do a quick case study of balance. Get up and stand on one leg, focusing on the way that your body weight pulls in several directions at once while being counterbalanced by your arm and shoulder movements, your hip positions, and the repositioning of your leg that's in the air. If you concentrate hard enough on trying to work out all of these feelings, motions, and positions, you'll probably end up falling over. With just balancing on one leg being too complicated and abstract to describe, how can we expect someone to be able to explain it to us for a motor movement or athletic motion? It's impossible but, unfortunately, that's exactly how many try to instruct us on the way to swing a golf club or throw a ball. We would do far better to *feel* our own balance than to try and recreate it through a mechanical description of how the move should be performed. In this section, we're going to add to your knowledge of proprioception that we covered back in Chapter 3. Let's begin by looking at the two highly advanced human skills of balance and coordination and defining the relationship between them that gives rise to our ability to perform beautifully complex motor movements.

The Relationship Between Balance and Coordination

As the fundamentals of body awareness and control, balance and coordination are responsible for how quickly, efficiently, and effectively we learn and perform our motor skills, as well as how well we can perform multiple motor movements at once or in succession. Developing your balance and coordination will not only help you to reach peak levels of performance, but will also ensure that you don't develop posture problems, significantly reduce the chances of you injuring yourself by falling over, and improve the responsiveness of your reflexes. Not only that, but balance and coordination also increase how strong we are, how flexible we are, and even how speedy we are, as well as contribute to our body's overall ability to act as a cohesive whole. Let's give you a quick definition of each before we move forward.

Balance can best be understood as our ability to maintain a certain position no matter the movement that we are performing. Coordination, on the other hand, refers to our body's ability to synchronize a number of different muscles and movements, unifying them together to perform a certain action. Because both of these are essential to movement, it's impossible to complete any action, sporting or otherwise, without correctly combining our balance with our coordination.

Exercises for Enhancing Balance and Coordination

As I'm sure you might have guessed, both balance and coordination are key determiners of how well you can perform motor movements which, in turn, determines how effective your actions are and what level of peak performance you can reach. While improving our balance increases our overall performance abilities, improving our coordination improves our specific performance abilities, such as the correctly ordered, directed, and executed combination of various motor movements. You need to synchronize both your body and actions in the way required to reach the level of the pros and excel in your chosen sport. Through a combination of enhanced balance and excellent coordination, you'll not only be able to complete motor movements more efficiently with greater levels of harmony and precision than ever before, but you'll also use less energy and spend less time doing so. Furthermore, improving these two facets of your body serves as the perfect complement to your physical prowess and fitness and strengthens your neuromuscular systems. Let's go over some of the main exercises you should include in your exercise routine to improve your balance and coordination:

- **Squats and Lunges**

As we covered in Chapter 3 when covering some exercises to improve your proprioception, squats are one of the most useful exercises to increase your stability and improve your balance, and they cost you nothing to do! You can squat it out anywhere, at any time. Stand with your feet hip-width apart, place your arms on the sides of your body, and, as you stick your butt out and bend your knees (making sure that they don't go further than your toes), raise your arms up until they are at eye level. Hold this position for 5 seconds before returning to the starting point, doing this between 8 and 10 times.

For lunges, start in the same position as with a squat. But, instead of bending both knees and sitting back as if into a chair, you're going to take a step forward with one leg. Bend the knee of the leg with which you step forward up while keeping your foot of this leg flat on the ground. Bend the knee of the other leg down so that it's almost touching the ground, keeping only your toes or the front of your foot on the ground. You can either step back up into the starting position and then repeat the movement with the other leg going forward this time, or you can lunge on the move, stepping forward before bending the knee with the other leg forward this time. Complete the same number of repetitions as for the squat.

- **Quadruped Position**

By quadruped position, I mean get into a push-up-like stance with your palms flat on the ground but with both of your knees on the floor. Make sure that your arms are shoulder-length apart and that your legs are hip-width apart. Then, raise one arm straight out in front of you and the opposite leg straight out behind you. Hold yourself in this position for around 10–15 seconds before returning to the quadruped position and repeating the action with the other arm and opposite leg. Aim for 6–8 repetitions for each arm and leg combo.

- **Heel Raises**

For heel raises, get into a similar position as for a squat, with your arms stretched down on your sides. Take a breath in, hold it, and then exhale slowly. As you breathe out, raise your arms up in front of you while simultaneously lifting up your heels. Once your arms are at eye level and heels are up, hold this position for about 15 seconds. Then, slowly lower yourself back into the starting position, and take a five-second breath in before exhaling again and repeating the motion. Aim for 10 repetitions.

Remember that balance and coordination are not skills that will improve overnight. You'll want to keep up these activities, as well as others, and practice them regularly to ensure you get the results you're after, as well as to help prevent injuries and improve your proprioception and bodily awareness. Take the secret of balance to heart and coordinate your brain and body together for the ultimate results. Remember that having good balance and coordination is a survival trait of the fittest humans, so if you want to become one of the fittest humans alive, or at least in your sport, aim to improve these two fundamental aspects of body awareness.

7

THE ICEMAN COMETH

When it comes to sports and performing at the highest of levels, you have to be both physically and mentally tough. You could say it almost goes with the territory. When battling it out in a competition or facing the pressure of a grueling training session, we have to endure. And, when things don't go as planned, which will happen more often than you'd like, you still have to find a way to come out on top. As pro athletes, we need to have ice in our veins; remain steely-eyed, with a stiff upper lip, and the heart of a lion no matter the circumstances.

Reaching peak performance on the regular starts with developing a resilient mindset. Most amateurs have a tendency to consider the mental side of sports as thinking through your technique or planning out your next move. But, as every pro knows, it's so much more than that. Let's say that your technique doesn't work out the way that you planned or that you just can't seem to get the hang of a specific move you need to take your game to the next level. The amateur will often dig themselves into a destructive hole, spiraling down into a state of despair through thoughts like "I'm just not good enough." The pro, on the other hand, knows that this type of destructive thinking does no good for anyone trying to improve their game because it gives power to the conscious mind.

As we have seen so far in this book, you want your conscious mind to be as inactive as possible while performing a motor movement, making it relinquish the driver's seat and rather fill the role of the observant passenger analyzing the route. The experienced athlete knows that they need their subconscious to take the wheel if they are to reach peak performance. As such, they develop a number of tools, techniques, and habits to ensure that their movements and actions reach the stage of automaticity as quickly and efficiently as possible so that they can rely less on the conscious and more on the subconscious. This is the mental strength of the pro.

In this chapter, we're going to go over some of the best habits you can develop for increasing your mental strength. We'll begin by covering how imagery and visualization can help to take your athletic performance to the next level before diving into the building blocks you can use to create an unbreakable mindset. It's time to learn how to mentally prepare yourself for reaching the level of the pro athlete—you're nearly there and, by the end of this chapter, you'll be even closer to achieving your goals!

MENTAL IMAGERY AND VISUALIZATION

One thing that almost all experienced athletes do as part of their practice sessions, before a game, or in the run-up to a major competition, is that they visualize how they want the game to go. This gives these athletes the competitive edge because they're *seeing* the tactics of their opponents, *feeling* the motor movements that they need to make to overcome these tactics, and even *hearing* the cheers of the crowd as they make that shot or swing and come out on top. Before the game's even begun, the elite athlete is already visualizing themselves as the winner. If nothing else, it means that they go into the game with the confidence of a champion, which is why they're twice as likely to defeat someone who's been fretting over whether they're good enough to be competing or worried about the fight they had with their girlfriend the night before. Even if two people have the same skill set, talent, and physical strength, it's the one that practices visualization techniques who will come out on top.

In sport, people tend to prefer using the term "mental imagery" rather than visualization. They pretty much mean the same thing, but whereas visualization is commonly used to refer to the mental practice of focusing on a single goal or outcome, imagery goes above and beyond that. By imagery, we are referring to the process by which an athlete pictures their entire performance, from beginning to end, using as many of the senses as they can to bring the game, practice, or competition to life in their minds. Athletes that employ the visualization technique of mental imagery develop the habit of heightened mental awareness which, in turn, increases their confidence, calms their mind, and through this, enhances their chances of reaching peak performance.

Mental Rehearsal Ups Your Game

By creating vivid, life-like images of the way that they want the game to go in their minds, athletes make clear to their subconscious what their intentions are. The subconscious can then use this detailed sensory information to make it reality. It might sound crazy, but mental rehearsal is a tried-and-tested technique that has been studied by sports psychologists for years. *And proven to work.* In fact, it doesn't matter how old you are, or what your current athletic abilities may be, using mental imagery and visualization has been shown to increase your skill sets, as well as to provide the cognitive and emotional levels needed to flow into the zone of peak performance.

When mentally rehearsing for your next practice session or game, try not to focus on the outcome goal of, for example, making the team cut or winning gold, but rather on the *process* goal. The way to think about it is like the cliché saying: "It's not about the destination, it's about the journey." Rather than visualizing yourself as having finished the practice session or having won the medal, you need to create imagery for the full picture, mentally rehearsing from the point of your last best performance that led you to this moment, to the way that stretching before the game will feel. Experience each motor movement as you get onto the field and begin the game, *feel* your exhilaration as you get one over on your competitors or successfully perform a particularly complicated action, work your way to the end of the game, and to achieving your desired outcome before returning to the present moment and living out that exact mental rehearsal in reality.

As with everything in sports, practice might not make us perfect (an impossible and unrealistic goal to set for yourself), but it does make you the best that you could be. You're going to need to repeat the technique of mental imagery time and time again until it becomes a skill in its own right. As with anything that you learn, it's not going to be easy at first and you're not going to create very vivid images straight away. But, keep on practicing it, focusing on the visual images, the kinesthetic (bodily) feelings, and the auditory cheers of the crowd. Trust me, this will give you the competitive edge you need to reach the levels of peak performance reserved for the pro athlete.

THE HABIT OF AN UNBREAKABLE MINDSET

We humans are creatures of habit. They are what define us and give our lives meaning, whether for the better or for the worse. Many habits of our minds are inhibitors of success that hold us back from reaching our true potential. Oftentimes, this is done by urging ourselves to be perfect and avoid making any and all mistakes. As a result of this, we end up becoming nervous, self-critical, doubtful, and too scared of getting something wrong to focus on getting it right. In other words, our habit of expecting the best from ourselves is often what leads us to perform worse. This is why it's essential that an athlete develop the habit of mental strength.

The Good, the Bad, and the Beautiful

There is far more to reaching peak performance than just the physical side of working out and practicing the moves. It's also vital to train your mind. Learning about the psychological side of athletic performance is what separates the amateurs from the elite, and allows the pros to reach their peak performance no matter the circumstances. In this section, we're going to go over the good, the bad, and the beautiful of how to develop an unbreakable mindset, why the average person fails to create one, and how to use focus and visualization to protect you against failure.

- **The Good**

Let's begin with covering the good news about developing an unbreakable mindset: anyone can do it. All you need to do is develop the habit of positive thinking. Most athletes only try to incorporate positive thinking come crunch time or when things go well. But, the pros know that developing positive thoughts and the skill of constructive criticism should be something that you practice in every training session. Because, believe it or not, thinking this way takes practice. You have to consciously focus your attention on thinking positively and show up to each and every practice with the attitude that what you are doing is the best way to become the greatest athlete you can be. This doesn't mean that you shouldn't, and won't, fail; it means that you change the way you view and think about failure. As Thomas Edison said about inventing the light bulb: "I have not failed. I've just found 10,000 ways that won't work." And, you know what, on the 10,001st time, Edison tried again and succeeded, changing the world as we know it.

Edison, like the pro athlete, knew that failure wasn't the end of the road or a signal that he should give up. It was just good feedback on what wasn't working, or on an area that needed to be focused on and improved upon. One of the best ways to develop the mental fortitude required to compete at the highest of levels is to leave behind the notion that we shouldn't fail or that failure is a shortcoming. In fact, how would we ever improve if we didn't have failure to show us exactly what needs to be improved? Embracing failure and developing the habit of positive thinking are two of the surest ways of boosting your confidence. Confidence, in turn, is what's needed to become mentally tough and develop an unbreakable mindset.

I'm sure that you've heard about athletes who seem to be able to push themselves beyond their limits when it really matters. Perhaps you've even seen them in action yourself. Well, I'm here to tell you that this performance is not a one-and-done for that athlete. In fact, it's just the very tip of the iceberg of their habit of not just believing that they have the competitive edge, but *knowing* that they do. How did they know this? They had put in the hard work of honing not only their body but also their mind in every practice session. They had failed countless times and used this failure to improve, helping to build them up not break them down. Their positive outlook on failure and on life, in general, had given them the thick skin needed to keep going during a practice session when all others were ready to call it quits. It is through this that they had sharpened the mental 'edge' needed to leave the competition eating their dust. This edge of a confident and unbreakable mindset was not something they pulled out of the bag during the competition or five minutes before it; it was the result of the way they approached each and every training session. So, the good news is that all you need to do to develop an unbreakable mindset is to *practice* having one.

• The Bad

Now that we've talked about the athlete's best weapon —confidence—and the good news that anyone can develop it, it's time to move on to the athlete's biggest threat—self-doubt—and the bad news that anyone can suffer from it. If they're not prepared to deal with it, that is. When we feel self-doubt, our minds tend to tense up and we find it difficult to think clearly or to concentrate. As a result of this, our bodies begin to tense up, too. Now, it's important to remember that confidence is not an -all-or-nothing kind of game, and we're all going to go through times when we begin to doubt ourselves and our abilities. But what separates the amateur from the elite athlete is that the pro is willing to acknowledge self-doubt as a passing phase or as a state of mind that needs to be dealt with, rather than viewing it as an irreversible condition that you can do nothing about but wallow in.

Treat self-doubt like a sickness of the mind. When we are sick, we take measures to combat the sickness, such as by taking medicine, in order to ensure that we return to peak health as quickly as possible. When you start to feel the onsets of self-doubt creeping into your mind, don't wallow it or expect it to clear up on its own. Take steps to combat it before it begins to eat away at your confidence. Develop techniques to motivate yourself such as through saying positive affirmations ("I am good, I am great. I am one badass athlete capable of doing anything I set my mind to"). Seek out someone who you know will lift you up when you're feeling down, such as your partner, family member, coach, or teammate, and ask them to give you a pick-up pep talk. Finally, remember why it is that you began doing your chosen sport in the first place and why you've spent so much time practicing and perfecting your skill in it... you love to play it! Expectations from yourself and from others will always make you feel a bit down, especially on an off day or as you start to climb the ranks of professionalism in the sport. Combat the self-doubt that might arise from this by reconnecting to your root reason for why you do what you do. Expectations come a far second to your love for the game.

- **The Beautiful**

With the athlete's top weapon of confidence and worst enemy of self-doubt outlined and defined, it's now time to turn to the beautiful news: Just as self-doubt kills confidence, so too does confidence slay self-doubt. With both killing the other one, it's up to you as the athlete to decide which one you give your power to. In other words, the beautiful thing is that it's up to you whether you let confidence or self-doubt reign supreme; you have the power and you have the choice. It's obviously a no-brainer which one you want to come out on top, so start acting like it and watch those self-doubts fall to the wayside.

There are certain things that you can do to ensure that your mind remains clean and clear of doubtful and acidic thoughts, as well as ways to ensure that you don't choke up when it comes time to perform at your peak for a major competition. As we spoke about when covering "The Bad" section above, all it takes is applying the right remedy or medicine to deal with the 'sickness'. Another beautiful thing is that it's way simpler than you think to do this. All you need to do is to develop the skill of remaining relaxed and focused. And, yes, these are skills, which means that they can, and should, be worked on and honed just like any other technique in your sport.

In order to focus the mind, you need to think *simply*. We humans are extremely complicated beings, and oftentimes these complications are of our own creation. We don't actually need to live such compli-cated lives, and we don't need to complicate matters when it comes to playing sports. Try and simplify what you're focusing on to one or two things at a time, and only focus on what is absolutely necessary. Do you need to review all of your shortcomings or flaws in your performance right before a competition or prac-tice? No! This is a sure way to complicate your mind, awaken self-doubt, and overwhelm yourself to the point that you choke up and fall far short of your peak performance. So, don't do it. Say a few positive affirma-tions before the game to boost your confidence levels rather than over-analyze past mistakes and walk onto the field already defeated by self-doubt.

Our brains seriously struggle to focus on more than two things at the same time. Although women may claim to be multitaskers and are better at it than men, it's still not the ideal situation to try and focus on a variety of different things at the same time. And, you need to aim for the ideal if you're to induce the flow state needed to reach peak performance. A good way to simplify complicated moves that you need to remember or changes in tactics that need to occur during the game is to use cue words. The funny phrases that you hear football coaches shouting at their teams to make clear a change in tactic or specific hand signals signed by baseball catchers and coaches aren't only done to ensure that their opponents don't know what's coming next. They're also done because such cues are a great way to condense a lot of complicated strategy into one simple, easily understood word, phrase, or hand sign. Through practicing such strategic maneuvers and connecting them with a simplified cue, all the brain of these players needs is to see or hear the cue to know exactly what to do without having to run through each and every instruction or step of the process. What was originally a string of commands has become one thing to focus on.

And, these types of cues don't only apply to team sports. Jake Clark, throws and strength coach and multi-sport athlete, summed it up perfectly when he said, "when I threw javelin in college, one thing I often tried to improve was the explosiveness of my block and throw. I regularly used "Tick-Tock Boom" (shorter than the reality of right foot, left foot, throw) as my cue words to help keep my focus on a fast final two steps and an explosive throw prior to my approach." At other times, Jake didn't even use words or phrases as his cue. A simple double clap would remind him that he needed to keep his final two steps done in quick succession. So, while practicing your motor movements or working on different complicated strategies, think of what you need to remember during the game and figure out a simplified cue that can encapsulate it and keep you focused.

You're also going to need to combine simplifying your focus with ways to relax. Like focus, feeling relaxed during a high-pressure situation comes from feeling confident, as well as helping you to feel more confident. But it can quickly become a vicious cycle of self-doubt if you start to become tense, nervous, or anxious and haven't worked on any techniques to calm yourself down. Have you ever noticed how almost all professional athletes seem to make even the most complicated of moves seem easy and effortless? Their motions are fluid and, at times, can even seem mesmerizing as they flow smoothly from one position to the next (the key word being 'flow', of course). If you've ever tried to replicate the actions of a pro, you'll know that, although they may make it look simple, it's anything but. It's just that they've practiced the movements so many times that they have automated the motor skill, switching off the self-doubting conscious mind in favor of the powerhouse of the subconscious. It's also because they've honed their ability to remain calm and composed while competing at the highest of levels. If you're physically tense while competing, it doesn't matter how mentally focused you may be, you're not going to flow into the zone of peak performance.

One of the best ways to relax your body and mind before a big game is to listen to calming music. Try to listen to the same type of music, or even the same song, every time so that your mind builds that connection between the music and the relaxed state of being. Contrary to popular belief, you want to keep your adrenaline levels low prior to stepping onto the field, so no heavy metal before the game. Unless that type of music calms you down, that is. Another great way to improve your ability to destress your body and mind before a competition is to develop a meditation practice. Like every other skill that helps you reach your peak performance, meditation takes work and a lot of training to get right. Entering into the meditative state where you can clear your mind isn't going to happen overnight, just like you didn't learn to do any other skill in your sport perfectly the first or even the tenth time. But, once you've mastered the skill of clearing your mind, you'll find your body naturally beginning to relax as soon as you close your eyes and start to meditate. Once this is done, add the technique of mental rehearsal and visualization that we covered in the previous section, and you're onto a winner of a pre-competition ritual.

Just like you wouldn't show up to a game without being physically fit and ready for the level of competition you're facing, you should never show up without being mentally fit and ready too. Practice the techniques of mental imagery and visualization, take a deep swig of self-confidence, and treat self-doubt like you would any other opponent that you have to defeat. Hone your focus and relax both body and mind, and you'll find yourself flowing into the zone of peak performance in no time, every time.

8

AN OPEN MIND AND A SEE-THROUGH HEART

I f your sport involves playing in a team, then you're going to need to develop an environment or ethos of trust, rapport, and cooperation. Getting to the stage of openness and inclusiveness required if a team is to reach peak performance as a single entity rather than as a group of self-interested individuals is quite a tough thing, especially considering that people often have hidden agendas for doing what they do. If you have to guess what the other players are thinking or are unsure of what their intentions are, then you are awakening that biggest opponent to the flow state and reaching peak performance: doubt.

In this chapter, we're going to cover some tips and techniques that will help you work effectively as a team. We'll begin by talking about something called radical transparency and how it leads to a transformative environment that leads to collaborative breakthroughs, increases team chemistry, and allows for all to share in the success that comes about from working as a cohesive unit. After that, we'll go over the main advantages of working as a team in sport, just to hit home the importance, and benefit, of putting aside your individual agenda for the good of the team. Remember, no one is meant to live in this world alone, and if you want to compete in a team sport at the highest of levels, you're going to need to reach peak performance as a group, not as a bunch of highly skilled individuals. In sports, teamwork really does make the dream work!

RADICAL TRANSPARENCY

Have you heard of the billionaire investor and hedge fund manager Ray Dalio before? Although he may not be an athlete, not by a long shot, one of his concepts—having a radically open mind through the use of radical transparency—is transferable to the world of sports. This concept helped Ray earn his billions, and it can help you to dramatically improve the collaboration of your team into a single lean, mean, competition-winning machine. When we embrace the idea of an open and transparent team environment, we become able to face and overcome the real problems that hinder working together. And, through the aim of reaching consensus with the other players, this is not done in a way that pits one against another in a battle of ideas or ideology. In order to succeed in team sports, you need to come to terms with the fact that you being right matters less than acting in a way that is best for the team. Now, this doesn't mean that disagreements should be hidden under the rug and allowed to fester, not at all. But it means that they should be dealt with in a way that Ray calls "healthy disagreement."

When we are completely transparent with one another, we feel comfortable voicing our ideas and opinions, even if we know that others may not agree with them. We have the confidence to discuss issues and to not try to polarize the debate, but rather work together to find a middle ground solution that's in the best interest of the team, not any individuals in it. This is the heart of radical transparency; to create a culture of being direct and trusting our team members to respect our opinions, even if they don't agree with them. It's about communicating honestly with the intent of improving the whole and forging deeper relationships than the surface level of practicing and playing together.

Now, the level of honesty and openness required for radical transparency can be difficult to obtain, for some people in the team more than for others. It takes courage to be able to speak out against someone with more confidence than you, or in a position of power such as a coach or team captain. It also takes some thick skin to be able to take someone critiquing your strategy or pointing out areas for you to improve without flying off the handle and yelling at them or feeling down-hearted and useless. But this is what it takes to compete with the pros, and it is also why Ray uses the word 'radical' in his term.

By definition, 'radical' means to take things as far as is possible. But it doesn't mean that you have to go overboard. That is, you don't have to go further than you need to. There's a difference between radical transparency and being unnecessarily hurtful. You need to work together as a team to decide where you draw the boundary line with your version of radical transparency, which is also a great way to begin creating your team culture. Use phrases like "Can I tell you what I really think about that?" or "Please tell me your honest opinion," as trigger warnings before diving in and being transparent. Through this system of honesty and openness, you'll not only build far deeper and more tight-knit relationships with your teammates, but will also gain insights into the ways that their minds work that can help you to know what their next move is going to be in a given situation. This is how you flow into the zone of peak performance as a team and not just as an individual. It will take quite a bit of effort at first to get radical transparency right, but the results are so worth it that they outweigh these efforts ten to one.

THE ADVANTAGES OF TEAMWORK

If there were no rules in a sport, it would be chaos out on the field. Similarly, if you don't take the time to define the rules of how your team culture operates and what roles individuals should play within the team, then the team structure will break down. When this happens, people start to act in their own self-interest almost as a defense mechanism, and the power of teamwork turns from realizing the dream into a nightmare. This is an all-too-common thing in modern sports today where strong personalities try to dominate the other members of the team. It's vital to keep in mind that no team is one-for-all, but rather should be all-for-one.

Learning how to be an integral part of a team is a vital asset that will serve you both on the field and off. With the right culture of encouragement, collaboration, openness, and honesty, a team can achieve wonders that are much greater than the sum of its parts. Let's go over some of the major benefits of teamwork in sports:

1. The Power of Cooperation

The first benefit of teamwork comes from the ability to cooperate with other people. This is a skill that reaches far beyond the sporting world to have a lasting impact on your ability to be an active member of your work team and of society at large. When you work together as a team, you learn how to keep personal differences or differences of opinion from impacting your ability to practice, play, and collaborate with one another. These differences are put to the side as you focus on what's best for the team rather than what's best for you. Through the power of cooperation, team members learn to look at the bigger picture and to realize that the whole is much more effective than the sum of its parts. This is a vital skill for team sports and for living a successful and rewarding life.

2. Develop Your Social Skills

One of the main reasons our parents encourage us to play sports as kids is to socialize with other people our age who may share the same or similar interests to us. This is especially true in sports where teamwork is needed, where we often have to leave behind our social shyness or awkwardness, get out of our comfort zone, and interact with the kinds of people you'd never have talked to if not for the fact that you were on the same team. Team sports often result in friendships that last for a lifetime, because it is vital to bond with the other members of your team if you're to play together successfully and reach the level of team flow.

3. Confidence-Building

By cooperating and socializing with your teammates, you'll also increase your self-confidence. Team sports is a renowned confidence booster, especially when the team plays as a unit and the players encourage one another to improve. This enhances our self-image and makes us feel like we are part of something bigger than just our own little existence.

4. A Little Healthy Competition Goes a Long Way

Playing a team sport can be a double whammy for healthy competition. Not only are you competing with each other to achieve a common goal, but you're also pushing one another to play and do better in the pursuit of team excellence. Team sports help us to get used to working hard and playing with others in a friendly but competitive way that sees everyone getting incrementally better. It also teaches us the value of humble victories and how to recover from losses.

5. Life Skills That Will Last You a Lifetime

Besides the skills covered above, there are loads more that playing team sports introduces into our lives. These include things like teaching us the best way to deal with conflict and how to resolve it correctly, accepting a variety of different viewpoints and expanding our worldview, and developing respect for other humans. It also greatly enhances our skills as a leader, as a goal-setter and getter, and as a self-disciplined and resilient individual.

6. Provides You with a Support System

Although most of us have a family that supports and encourages us, not all of us are that lucky. For those that don't have the most supportive of families, their team members can stand in their place, providing encouragement, and serving as a pillar of strength to help them get through trying times. The most successful teams aren't only there for each other on the field, but off the field too.

And, there you have it, folks. A short and sweet chapter on the massive benefits that playing in a team sport has on our lives and livelihoods. Even if you don't play in a team, you can still surround yourself with other players of your sport that, through a little healthy competition, can help you to reach the next level of your progress and performance. Remember that no man (or woman) is an island and we all need support structures in our lives. Besides the physical strength and mental well-being that playing sports provides us with, it can also serve as our way to improve our social skills too. Now, time to move on to the final chapter in this book, where we'll chat about one of the most important people in the lives of any player: your coach.

9

PUT ME IN, COACH!

One of the hallmarks of skill development in sports is to have a coach show you the ropes. A coach is the person who has given up or puts second for the duration of the practice, their own attempts to perfect their form in order to analyze and develop those of you and your team. They provide the unambiguous feedback required to make improvements using their experiential knowledge, combining it with their observations. They provide encouragement and enforce the training regimens that keep you in the best mental and physical states possible to reach peak performance.

A great coach is an excellent asset to any and every athlete, especially if they share some of the same philosophies and outlook on life. There's also no one better positioned to help identify what issues you need to address to take your game to the next level or to point out things that you may not have otherwise been aware of or capable of observing. As we said in the paragraph above, it's not only your physical prowess that a great coach can help you to hone, but the as-important factor of mental strength. They can guide you through the process of mental rehearsal and visualization, or give you the insider information needed to re-create actual game situations, settings, and feelings. Finally, a great coach is someone who you know is on your side and is invested in you becoming the best that you can be at the sport that you love. This provides a pillar of non-parental support that is not experienced in many walks of life outside of the sporting world.

As you might have guessed by now, this chapter is dedicated to that figure in the background of every great athlete: the coach. After looking into some coaching strategies used to maximize long-term learning and performance, we'll turn to how coaches help us to tap into our best physical form and to develop the state of mind needed to flow into the zone of peak performance. Put me in, coach!

COACHING THE RIGHT WAY

While a lot of athletes might believe that it's the quantity of practice that you put in that pays off with reaching peak performance, this is not the case. If you think that all you have to do is to reach 10,000 hours and you'll automatically be a pro, I've got some bad news for you, because this just isn't the case. As the world of sports science has improved and developed, sports scientists have realized that it's a lot more to do with the *quality* of the practice time that you put in, rather than just the quantity.

One of the big breakthroughs in coaching and sports science of recent times is the difference between short-term and long-term motor skill improvement. In the traditional way of coaching and practicing, the athlete would be told to do the same repetitive drill over and over again to solidify the motor patterns, while the coach barks corrective feedback at the players whenever they see something that they think needs to be done better, or when they see a player slacking off. But, while this coaching strategy might result in short-term improvements in performance during that specific practice session, it does not result in lasting motor skill improvement that carries over to the next training session, to the competition, and beyond.

Long-Term Learning vs. Short-Term Performance

Long-term motor learning results in, as the name implies, pretty much permanent improvement and is generally measured according to an athlete's ability to perform said motor skill outside of regular practice (i.e. during matches or competitions).

It's vital that a coach understand the difference between learning and performance, and all of the factors that are involved in both. Let's go over some of the main factors that affect how an athlete learns, as well as how coaches can use these to their advantage:

- **Learner Autonomy**

While a coach is there to guide athletes in improving their skill sets and structuring their training regiments, a coach should never try to dictate to, or overly control, those they are coaching. In fact, having autonomy and feeling like you have a choice is a natural motivation booster, increasing our performance by making it our own. And, when we improve our motor skills while feeling like we are doing it of our own volition, this is one helluva confidence booster too. The best coaches give their athletes some control over specific parts of the practice, such as how to begin the training sessions, the order that the drills are carried out, and how often they require to be given a demonstration of how the motor movement is meant to look or work.

Research has shown that learner autonomy not only helps to improve learning of that specific motor skill, but even of skills that are unrelated to the choice that the athlete made. A simple example of how this can work comes from golf, where a study was conducted on giving players the choice of which color golf ball they practiced putting with. This seemingly irrelevant factor resulted in those who were given the choice outputting those who were not on the day. Not only this but when their long-term motor skill improvement was tested a day or two later, those with the choice were observed to have retained far more of the improvement than the other test group. The bottom line: learner autonomy, whether directly relevant to the motor skill or not, has a positive effect on motor learning.

- **Feedback and Focus**

As we spoke about in the introduction to this chapter, the traditional, stereotypical, image of a coach is someone barking commands from the sidelines. But, this is more often than not detrimental to the attentional focus of the athlete, especially during a high-stakes competition. Knowing when to give and how to vocalize feedback is an invaluable skill for a coach to develop. Once again, embracing autonomy and letting the athletes themselves select when they wish to receive feedback has been proven to improve motor learning and skill retention. If a coach has to give feedback from the sidelines, then barking commands is definitely not the way to do it. A more positive form of vocalization always gets the message across more effectively and with longer-lasting results.

And don't forget to also point out when the players are doing well! As the people critiquing the athletes in order to help them improve, coaches tend to be overly critical when it comes to the feedback that they give. This can once again negatively impact a player's confidence and their ability to remain focused on the game, as they are continuously worried that their coach is going to shout out their flaws. This is a big killer of an athlete being able to activate flow state in a game or competition. A coach should think about the timing of their feedback and focus on giving solutions, putting more emphasis on positive comparisons and on the external goals than on negative comparisons and internal body movements.

- **Practice Schedules**

One of the main trademarks of coaching is to provide athletes with the practice exercises that they need to succeed and reach the next levels of their performance. There are two main types of practice schedules that great coaches make use of: blocked practice and random practice. Blocked practice schedules are the ones that coaches have traditionally used and involve blocking out, or 'chunking', different skills or parts of a motor movement to be practiced and improved separately before joining it all together. This type of practice scheduling means that there is low interference from the context (such as using this skill in an actual game-play setting) or from the environment (such as having to compete with other players while performing the motor movement), and has been shown to be effective for improving an athlete's performance of the motor skill, especially when they are first starting out with the motor movement or with the sport. Random practice scheduling can be considered the opposite of the blocked scheduling method, as it involves throwing the athlete into the deep end by providing them with a lot of interference from the context (such as free play or a mock game against teammates) or environment (trying to emulate challenges that an athlete would come across in competition settings). Random practice schedules have been shown to enhance an athlete's learning and long-term retention of the motor skill, as it forces them to adapt to challenging or changing situations. It also allows the athlete to develop a deeper understanding of the way that the motor movement works and how to use it in actual gameplay, rather than viewing it as a repetitive motion carried out in a controlled setting.

Let's use an example from the world of basketball to show you how these two practice schedules weigh up against one another. In a study conducted on high-school basketball players, researchers separated the participants into two groups. The first was given a blocked practice schedule involving chest passes, overhead passes, and sidearm passes. The other group was told to practice these same kinds of passes but in the form of a mock game. During the practice session, the blocked practice group was recorded to outperform the random practice group and displayed better performance of the motor skills being tested. The random practice group also displayed more frustration at not being able to get the motor movements right and felt like they weren't improving quickly enough. But, when the two groups came together the next day to practice the same kinds of throws, the random practice group performed better than the blocked practice group, showing that they had retained more learning of the motor skill. Furthermore, when the researchers changed up the context by making the participants increase the distance of the throws, the random practice group once again outperformed their blocked schedule counterparts.

So, what does this tell us about the way to arrange practice schedules? A balance of blocked and random schedules works best, with more blocked practice being done when first learning a motor skill or starting out at a new sport. Then, increase the amount of random practice carried out while providing positive feedback to keep the players from getting frustrated or demotivated. This is the best way to balance out short-term performance with long-term learning of a motor skill.

CONCLUSION

Welcome to the end of our journey into the world of how to flow into the zone of peak performance! We've gone through quite the learning journey together, covering everything that you need to know to turn you into the pro athlete that both you and I know that you not only are but deserve to be.

Let's go over a final quick review of some of the major themes we've covered in this here book, providing you with the key takeaways to refresh your mind and ensure you're in the ideal position to improve your skills and excel in your sport. It's time to look at the bigger picture of the nine powerful principles for reaching the peak of high performance in sports!

1. The Big Problem: Learning to Trust Your Mind

The first principle that we covered way back in Chapter 1 was to do with breaking you free of the misconception that improving in your sport is all about learning the physical skills. As we saw, and have seen throughout this book, that just isn't the case. We may be lean, mean, fighting machines, but we aren't clunky contractions of scrap metal. In order to reach peak performance, you need to approach motor learning in a way that combines both body and mind, with your aim to automate the process as much as possible as you get better at it. This is skills acquisition 101.

2. Turn Your Autopilot on and Enter the Flow State

Our next principle carried on from the first, outlining how it's not our entire minds that we need to trust in, but specifically our subconscious. The power of our subconscious minds is greater than we could ever have believed. Unlike our conscious mind, the subconscious doesn't hinder or handicap us by over-analyzing, being overly critical, or getting distracted by the smallest thing. It is through empowering our subconscious minds that we can automate our motor skills and flow into the zone of peak performance.

3. Do You Feel Like I Do? A.K.A., the Power of Proprioception

The third breakthrough principle for high performance in sports has to do with developing your proprioception. As we saw in Chapter 3, proprioception has to do with our ability to sense our body positions and predict the best movements to make in a given situation. Enhanced proprioception means that you are completely aware of your body and the various ways that it feels its way through actions and movements. Our proprioceptors are what tell us how much pressure, force, speed, or flexing you need to apply and do to complete a certain activity. This is what makes proprioception the pro athlete's sixth sense.

4. Trust Me, I Know What I'm Doing (The Power of Paying Attention)

In order to reach the peak of your performance, you need to learn how to focus your attention in the right way. As we saw in Chapter 4, having an external attentional focus where you're focused on the goal you want to achieve or the target you want to hit, rather than on trying to control your body to hit it, is another key principle for improving your performance. Remember to set SMART goals, making them specific, measurable, achievable, relevant, and time-based, and you are well on your way to becoming a pro in your sport.

5. Observe, Dear Watson, the Way to Let it Happen, Not Make it Happen

Sport is not about forcing yourself to do certain motor movements. If you try to make something happen, you will surely not get the results that you're looking for. This is because making things happen has to do with the conscious mind and, as we spoke about time and again in this book, being conscious of every move that you make is not the way to reach peak performance. In fact, it's the way to ensure that you don't enter into the flow state. After you mentally rehearse the motor movement and focus your attention on hitting your target or achieving your goal, let your subconscious mind take the wheel, observe the results, and use this unambiguous feedback to improve *after* the movement, not during it.

6. The Secret of Balance

The ability to balance is a trait of human evolution. It is one of the most phenomenal skills that we possess and has only been passed down through the fittest of our ancestors (because those without advanced balance generally died before procreating). Developing an in-depth understanding of the relationship between balance and coordination is key if you are to pass the test of survival of the fittest needed to reach the level of a pro athlete.

7. The Iceman Cometh: The Power of Mental Imagery and Visualization

The seventh principle for athletes to improve and excel in their sport is to develop the practice of mentally rehearsing the movements that they make, using as many of the five senses as possible to create an image in their minds of how they are going to achieve their goal or, better yet, how they have already done it. It is through viewing yourself as the pro athlete that you know you already are that you develop the unbreakable mindset needed to become one.

8. An Open Mind and a See-Through Heart

In order to develop the unbreakable mindset of a pro athlete, you're also going to want to develop the skill of radical transparency. This isn't only about being radically transparent with yourself and accepting of your failures and shortcomings as key parts of your learning journey, but also about being radically transparent with your teammates. Many sports require you to play in a team and, if your chosen sport is one of these, you have to learn to put the good of the team above your own self-interest. Remember that the whole is better than the sum of its parts!

9. Put Me in, Coach!

The final principle to improving and excelling in your sport is dedicated to those people who ensure that we get there. Every sport has a coach in some way or form, and their impact on not only our performance but on our lives and livelihood, cannot be understated. As long as they're coaching us in the right way, that is. Make sure that your coach understands how to motivate you in the right way, as well as knows the difference between blocked practice schedules and random practice schedules and the way to balance the two.

With the nine principles summarized, we are now done with this breakthrough book on how to become the best athlete that you could possibly be. But your journey isn't over just yet. Now that you have the tools, it's time to go out and put them to use! And, if you enjoyed this book and found the principles covered inside useful, please make sure to leave a review on Amazon so that others can benefit from it, too!

REFERENCES

Ablon, A. (2021). *The Subconscious Athlete's Mind Power*. Medium. https://april-76876.medium.com/the-subconscious-athletes-mind-power-5a1765ef1b20

AUSA Facility. (2022). *SMART Goals for Athletes*. AUSA FACILITY. https://www.ausafacility.com/blog/smart-goals

Bergland, C. (2021). *Why Letting Go of Self-Control Ups Your Game*. Www.psychologytoday.com. https://www.psychologytoday.com/us/blog/the-athletes-way/202108/why-letting-go-self-control-ups-your-game

Bogart, D. V. (2018). *Proprioception- The Sixth Sense That Every Athlete Needs To Develop*. Desired Health Chiropractic. https://www.desiredhealthchiro.com/2018/10/29/proprioception-the-sixth-sense-that-every-athlete-needs-to-develop/

Bourne, K. (2016). *Why is goal setting important*. Believe Perform. https://believeperform.com/why-is-goal-setting-important/

Cappello, K. (2019). *How to Get in the Zone*. Www.sportpsychologytoday.com. https://www.sportpsychologytoday.com/sport-psychology-for-athletes/how-to-get-in-the-zone-mindfulness/

Clark, J. (2022). *Sport Psychology 101: Building Blocks of an Unbreakable Mind*. Just Fly Sports. https://www.just-fly-sports.com/sport-psychology-101/

Elliott, L., & Wattie, N. (2020). *Coaching Strategies to Maximize Long-Term Learning and Performance for Athletes*. The Sport Information Resource Centre. https://sirc.ca/blog/learning-performance-distinction/

Enorcerna. (2022). ▷ *The 10 types of coordination (and their characteristics)*. Enorcerna. https://enorcerna.com/wiki/neurology/the-10-types-of-coordination-and-their-characteristics/#nav-2

García, M. J. (2021). *Coordination and Balance: Important, but underworked skills*. Blog about Fitness, Nutrition, Health, and Sport | HSN

Blog. https://www.hsnstore.eu/blog/sports/fitness/coordination-balance/

Gray, R. (2015). *How Do We Become an Expert? Intro to Skill Acquisition.* The Perception & Action Podcast. https://perceptionaction.com/8-2/

Hammett, G. (2018). *The Ugly Side of Transparency Ray Dalio on Radical Transparency.* Incafrica.com. https://incafrica.com/library/gene-hammett-3-steps-ray-dalio-uses-radical-transparency-to-build-a-billion-dollar-company

Hardy, B. (2016). *How To Learn A New Skill Well Enough To Do It Automatically.* Fast Company. https://www.fastcompany.com/3058572/how-to-learn-a-new-skill-well-enough-to-do-it-automaticall

Houston, E. (2019). *11 Activities and Exercises to Induce a Flow State.* PositivePsychology.com. https://positivepsychology.com/flow-activities/

iResearchNet. (2016, October 19). *Sports Psychology Flow.* IResearchNet. https://psychology.iresearchnet.com/papers/sports-psychology-flow/

Juma, N. (2022). *Thomas Edison Quotes on Greatness and Innovation.* Everyday Power. https://everydaypower.com/thomas-edison-quotes/

Kal, E., Prosée, R., Winters, M., & van der Kamp, J. (2018). Does implicit motor learning lead to greater automatization of motor skills compared to explicit motor learning? A systematic review. *PLOS ONE, 13*(9), e0203591. https://doi.org/10.1371/journal.pone.0203591

Martin, M. (2017). *Golgi Tendon Organs and Muscle Spindles Explained.* Www.acefitness.org. https://www.acefitness.org/fitness-certifications/ace-answers/exam-preparation-blog/5336/golgi-tendon-organs-and-muscle-spindles-explained/

Mayo Foundation. (2022). *Balance exercises: Step-by-step guide.* Mayo Clinic. https://www.mayoclinic.org/healthy-lifestyle/fitness/multimedia/balance-exercises/sls-20076853?s=5

Miller, K. D. (2019). *The Psychology and Theory Behind Flow.* PositivePsychology.com. https://positivepsychology.com/theory-psychology-flow/

Moore, C. (2019). *What is Flow in Psychology?* PositivePsychology.com. https://positivepsychology.com/what-is-flow/

Neumann, D. L. (2019). A Systematic Review of Attentional Focus Strategies in Weightlifting. *Frontiers in Sports and Active Living, 1*(7). https://doi.org/10.3389/fspor.2019.00007

Neuroscience, H. (2016). *The Athlete's Guide to the Brain: Motor Skill Learning.* Medium. https://blog.haloneuro.com/the-athlete-s-guide-to-the-brain-motor-skill-learning-43b4de7bd71d

Oliver, K. (2015). *Best Knee Strengthening Exercises to Relieve Pain.* Dr. Axe. https://draxe.com/fitness/knee-strengthening-exercises/

Oliver, K. (2016). *4 Proprioception Exercises for Balance and Strength.* Dr. Axe. https://draxe.com/fitness/proprioception/

Peterson, D. (2020). *Practice Really Does Change An Athlete's Brain.* 80 Percent Mental. http://www.80percentmental.com/blog/0percent mental.com/2012/12/practice-really-does-change-athletes.html

Quinn, E. (2021). *How Imagery and Visualization Can Improve Athletic Performance.* Verywell Fit. https://www.verywellfit.com/visualiza tion-techniques-for-athletes-3119438

Shaw, W. (2021a). *Motor Learning Explained.* Sportscienceinsider.com. https://sportscienceinsider.com/motor-learning/

Shaw, W. (2021b). *The Three Stages of Learning – Cognitive, Associative & Autonomous.* Sport Science Insider. https://sportscienceinsider.com/stages-of-learning/

Singh, H. (2019). *Skill Acquisition.* Science for Sport. https://www.scienceforsport.com/skill-acquisition/